NATIONAL ISSUES FORUMS

The bicentennial of the Bill of Rights provides a particularly timely occasion for reexamining the First Amendment and the civics lesson it was intended to teach. James Madison, Thomas Jefferson, and the others who framed the Bill of Rights were products of the Enlightenment era. Among other things, the First Amendment expressed a characteristic theme of that era by questioning authority. By guaranteeing free speech the First Amendment guards against the tendency of government to silence individuals who oppose the way official power is used.

Reflecting the emphasis of the Enlightenment era on the power of reason, the First Amendment recognizes the importance of a well-informed public. To the framers of the Bill of Rights, however, the concept of an informed public had a slightly different meaning than the one we attach to that phrase. In the Enlightenment era, being well informed meant having certain factual information — but it also meant thoughtfulness and the exercise of judgment.

Free speech is essential in a democratic nation, the framers of the Bill of Rights were convinced, because reaching public judgment requires considering various perspectives and comparing our views against opposing perspectives. The First Amendment serves as a reminder that a wide range of points of view must be presented in the marketplace of ideas to enable us, as citizens, to reach public judgment.

Those of us who have been involved over the past ten years in the National Issues Forums (NIF) — a nationwide consortium of citizens who come together in community Forums for nonpartisan discussion about public issues — have taken that lesson to heart. In this issue book, we examine the pros and cons of several points of view on free speech and when and how it should be restricted.

At a time of growing public concern about words and images that are racist, inflammatory, or pornographic, freedom of expression has become a prominent issue on the public agenda. But there is reason for concern about the tone of public discussion about free speech and how communities should respond when confronted with words and images that many people find offensive.

As Donald Downs, a political scientist at the University of Wisconsin, says in a recent book, *The New Politics of Pornography*, "Activists on all sides in the recent debate have often taken emotional and polarizing stands. Neither anti-porn activists nor anti-censorship liberals have shown much willingness to understand their opponents' concerns. There has simply been a clash of views. The extreme positions have demeaned the quality of public discourse on this issue and have jeopardized the quality of democratic debate."

Our purpose in this issue book on freedom of expression — and in public Forums on this topic — is not to advocate any single solution or point of view. It is, rather, to encourage constructive debate in which various perspectives are taken seriously. Our goal is to provide occasions in which concerned citizens can discuss this contentious issue, air their differences, think them through, and work toward acceptable solutions.

Our topic here — offensive speech and the measures some people favor to restrict it — has posed a dilemma for us as writers and editors. Paraphrasing offensive words or lyrics frequently sanitizes them, leaving some people to wonder what the fuss is about. To convey why there is growing sentiment for restricting certain kinds of speech, it is occasionally necessary — in our judgment — to quote such material directly. We apologize in advance for the discomfort this may cause some readers and trust that readers will understand our reasons for doing so.

After the Forums meet each year, the NIF convenes meetings with policymakers to convey the outcome of the discussions. So we can convey participants' thoughts and feelings about this issue, two ballots are included at the end of this book. Before you begin reading these materials, and then again after you have read them and taken part in Forums, I urge you to fill out these ballots and mail them back to us.

This book, like the others in this series, is a guide to one of the nation's pressing issues and an invitation to engage in public discussion and debate about it.

Keith Melville

Keith Melville, Managing Editor

Managing Editor: Keith Melville
Writer: Keith Melville
Research: Bill Carr
Editors: Harris Dienstfrey,
          Betty Frecker
Ballots: Amy Richardson,
          John Doble
Production Manager:
          George Cavanaugh

Designer: Greg Sundberg Design
Circulation Coordinator:
          Victoria Simpson
Cover Illustration: David Gothard
Word Processing: Valerie Breidenbach
Formatting: Christopher Baron,
          Jenifer Williams
Graphic Research: Bill Carr
Production Director: Robert E. Daley

The books in this series are prepared jointly by the Public Agenda Foundation —
a nonprofit, nonpartisan organization devoted to research and education about
public issues — and by the Kettering Foundation. They are used by civic and educational organizations interested in addressing public issues.

In particular, they are used in local discussion groups that are part of a nationwide network, the National Issues Forums (NIF). The NIF consists of thousands
of civic and educational organizations — colleges and universities, libraries, service
clubs, and membership groups. Although each community group is locally
controlled, NIF is a collaborative effort. Each year, convenors choose three issues
and use common materials — issue books such as this one, and parallel audio and
videotape materials.

Groups interested in using the NIF materials and adapting its approach as part of
their own program are invited to write or call for further information: National
Issues Forums, 100 Commons Road, Dayton, Ohio 45459-2777. Phone 1-800-433-
7834.

This edition is published by McGraw-Hill, Inc., 1221 Avenue of the Americas,
New York, New York 10020. For information or phone orders, call 1-800-338-3987.
Two other titles are available in this series:

Energy Options: Finding a Solution to the Power Predicament
America's Role in the World: New Risks, New Realities

THE BOUNDARIES OF FREE SPEECH: HOW FREE IS TOO FREE?

PREPARED BY THE PUBLIC AGENDA FOUNDATION

CONTENTS

TOXIC TALK: DEFENDING OURSELVES AGAINST OFFENSIVE MESSAGES

"The air and the airwaves are filled with crude language and caustic messages, and there is renewed debate about where to draw the line. When faced with offensive messages, how should communities respond?"

A question for America in the 1990s: Is there anything that cannot be said publicly, and *is* not being said? Freedom of expression is on the front burner as a public issue today because of growing concern that literally anything goes, no matter how tasteless, offensive, or socially corrosive. As the air and the airwaves are increasingly filled with crude language and caustic messages, there is growing concern about freedom of expression and renewed debate about where the line should be drawn that restrains or prohibits certain kinds of speech.

"In a society where anything goes, everything eventually will," says John Underwood, a feature writer for the *Miami Herald*. "We are being desensitized to almost every form of degenerate behavior. Giving in to the lowest common denominator is not what freedom of expression is all about. Freedom is not just about doing and saying whatever one pleases, but also about responsibilities for the common welfare. It is about exercising our right not to put up with the depravities that weigh us down."

Consider, for example, how much has changed in the messages conveyed by popular entertainers. A generation ago, when comedian Lenny Bruce used obscenity in his comedy routines, he was branded "the sickest comic of them all" by *Time* magazine. Despite the fact that Bruce justified his use of such language as a way of questioning traditional boundaries, his routines led to his conviction for public obscenity in 1964. Because of their explicit lyrics, rock 'n' roll performers Little Richard and Chuck Berry also faced legal reprisals.

Today, because of more permissive social norms, popular entertainers are freer to say what they want. Compared to recent offerings, Chuck Berry and Little Richard seem pretty tame. In the lyrics of rappers and rockers, in HBO comedy routines, and on radio where "shock jocks" specialize in school yard humor, there is something to offend everyone who is not Teflon-coated.

There is no question that crude language and gratuitous violence are more common today. New forms of sexually explicit expression — including "dial-a-porn" telephone services, X-rated videocassettes, and X-rated computer software — have proliferated. Moreover, there is reason for concern that sexually explicit material has become more hard-core, and that offensive messages have become more common in film, in daytime soap operas as well as prime-time television, in the lyrics of music groups, and in comedy routines.

Describing this situation, *Time* magazine writer Richard Corliss observes, "There's an acrid tang in nearly every area of American pop culture. Heavy metal masters Motley Crue invoke images of satanism and the Beastie Boys mime masturbation on stage. Rap poets like N.W.A. and the 2 Live Crew call for the fire of war against police or the brimstone of explicit, sulfurous sex. Comedians like Sam Kinison and Howard Stern bring locker-room laughs to cable TV and morning radio. On network TV, sitcom moms get snickers with innuendos about oral sex. In movies, the F-word has become so common, like dirty wallpaper, that the industry's conservative ratings board doesn't even bother to punish the occasional use of it with an R-rating."

Welcome to the no-holds-barred 1990s. In the words of Andrew Dice Clay, whose raw, stag-party jokes have made him one of the most prominent purveyors of the new comic raunch, "It's a new decade, and I got new filth for you."

AS NASTY AS THEY WANNA BE

Popular music is an especially vivid example of what has changed. Rock lyrics have long been raunchy and rebellious but, in recent years, rockers and rappers have become noticeably rawer. In 1957, producers of the "Ed Sullivan Show" were so concerned about Elvis Presley's pelvic gyrations that they instructed camera crews to shoot him from the waist up. Today, rock star Madonna — featured in a crotch-grabbing pose on the cover of a 1990 issue of *Interview* magazine — is pushing the limits farther. When she simulated an autoerotic orgasm on stage in her recent "Blonde Ambition" tour, HBO chose to broadcast the concert unexpurgated.

"Things have gotten out of control," says Joanne Masokowski, founder and director of a California organization called the Bay Area Citizens Against Pornography. It is only by exposing ourselves to some offensive words and messages, Masokowski says, that we can understand the extent of the problem. To illustrate her point, she refers to the lyrics of a 2 Live Crew rap song entitled "S and M." By her count, it contains 117 explicit references to male genitals, and oral sex is mentioned 87 times. The word "bitch" is used more than 100 times, and "fuck" occurs no fewer than 226 times. As if that were not enough, says Masokowski, the song also refers to feces, incest, urination, group sex, and violent sexual contact.

In recent months, Masokowski's organization has received an increasing number of phone calls from parents concerned about messages contained in popular entertainment. "There has to be some moderation here," says Masokowski. "It can't keep going in the direction it's been going for the past ten years."

The titles of cuts on 2 Live Crew's album, *As Nasty as They Wanna Be* — which include "Bad Ass Bitch,"

"Dick Almighty," and "Me So Horny" — help to explain why many people are offended. Although 2 Live Crew is notoriously crude, the group is hardly alone in its raw mixture of sex and violence. Listen, for example, to the words of the heavy metal group Guns 'N' Roses. In a track entitled "One in a Million," which begins "Immigrants and faggots, they make no sense to me, . . ." the group spreads an offensive gospel of intolerance and seems to be saying it's OK to hate entire groups of people.

HATE SPEECH ON CAMPUS

Popular entertainment is just one area in which offensive messages have prompted new concern about the acceptable limits of free speech. On college campuses across the country, there has been a disturbing upward trend in incidents of hate speech. Hundreds of campus bias incidents reported in recent years range from mildly threatening taunts and epithets to physical harassment. Many groups have been targeted, particularly blacks, Asians, Jews, male homosexuals, and lesbians.

In the spring of 1988 at Northern Illinois University, for example, a black student leaving a campus bar was confronted by students who yelled, "Niggers go home!" and "Niggers, we ought to lynch you!" At the University of Delaware in October 1988, campus sidewalks were defaced with anti-gay

slogans, including "Step Here, Kill a Queer," and "Stay in the Closet, Fag." At the University of Kansas, the B'nai B'rith Foundation received a letter reading "Jew-Boy, get out" and had a sign taped on its door that said "I'm gonna burn your Torah."

These are not isolated examples. Various organizations that monitor such incidents agree on the upward trend in recent years. For example, the National Institute Against Prejudice and Violence, a nonprofit group based in Baltimore, identified 174 campuses on which bias-motivated incidents occurred between September 1986 and December 1988, and by the end of 1990 the number had increased to 300. The National Gay and Lesbian Task Force, the Anti-Defamation League of B'nai B'rith, and the U.S. Department of Justice all find a similar trend in incidents of hate speech and racial tensions at institutions of higher education.

In a widely publicized incident, Brown University expelled student Douglas Hann in February 1991 for shouting racial epithets as well as abusive statements about Jews and gays in a late-night outburst in a campus courtyard. A student-faculty discipline committee decided that Hann had crossed the line separating hateful speech and "fighting words," and found him guilty of showing "flagrant disrespect for the well-being of others." It is the policy of Brown University, said President Vartan Gregorian, "to take action against those who incite hatred."

DRAWING THE LINE

Because of widely shared concern that toxic messages are engulfing the mainstream and polluting it, there is growing support for various measures to restrict offensive utterances. On campus, for example, in an effort to curb hate speech and discriminatory harassment, more than 100 American colleges and universities have taken steps to restrict offensive forms of expression, and to deal with what the National Institute Against Prejudice and Violence calls ethnoviolence, a comprehensive term that includes various acts of verbal harassment.

University officials defend speech codes as necessary measures to preserve and protect pluralism. The new rules about campus speech, says University of Wisconsin President Kenneth Shaw, are a way of "sending a message to minority students that the board and the administrators of this university do care." In the words of Emory University's director of equal opportunity, "I don't believe freedom of speech on campus was designed to allow people to demean others on campus."

Campus speech codes are just one of the measures taken to restrict bigoted messages. In 1990, New York *Newsday* columnist Jimmy Breslin was temporar-

Andrew Dice Clay: Pushing the limits in the no-holds-barred 1990s.

ily suspended from his job for making remarks to a colleague that were both racist and sexist. Andy Rooney, a TV commentator on "60 Minutes," was similarly suspended for several weeks after he made unflattering comments about blacks and gays.

At the level of government action, federal agencies have taken measures to restrict offensive speech. The FBI, the Justice Department, and the U.S. Postal Service have all launched aggressive anti-porn campaigns, threatening offenders with prosecution, steep fines, and confiscation of property. The Federal Communications Commission has recently been warning radio disc jockeys to clean up their acts and it has cracked down on a dozen radio stations, fining them for broadcasting offensive programming.

State legislatures and city governments have also gotten into the act. The Pennsylvania House of Representatives is considering a bill that would require a parental warning on offensive recordings. If record companies refuse to put warning labels on potentially offensive albums, Pennsylvania legislators are considering a measure that would prohibit the sale of recordings that describe or advocate suicide, incest, bestiality, sadomasochism, or rape, as well as messages that encourage murder or ethnic intimidation. Similar bills are under consideration in other states.

In October 1990, Cincinnati — a city whose strict anti-porn laws do not permit so-called adult book stores, peep shows, or X-rated movie houses — was the setting of the first obscenity case ever brought against a museum. Dennis Barrie, director of the Contemporary Arts Center, was indicted on charges of pandering obscene photographs. At issue was a controversial exhibition by Robert Mapplethorpe, including five

> "Whether the topic is racist epithets, raunchy pop lyrics, or offensive art, the question is how a community should respond, and whether censorship is appropriate."

photos depicting men in sadomasochistic poses and two showing nude children. Jurors were asked to decide whether the photographs appeal to prurient interest, whether they describe patently offensive sexual conduct, and whether they have serious artistic merit.

In June 1990, a Florida judge for the first time declared the lyrics of a recording obscene. U.S. District Court Judge Jose Gonzalez in Fort Lauderdale banned the 2 Live Crew album *As Nasty as They Wanna Be* on the grounds that it is offensive to the community. In the opening lines of his ruling, Judge Gonzalez commented that the case was "a battle between two ancient enemies, anything goes and enough already."

Several days after Judge Gonzalez's decision, which was binding in three counties in Florida, two members of the band were arrested for performing parts of the album in a concert date. Although most local stores quickly removed the album from their shelves, record store owner Charles Freeman was arrested on obscenity charges for selling the album. At Freeman's trial in October, Leslie Robson, an assistant state attorney, argued that free speech is not an absolute right: "The First Amendment does not give you the right to say what you want, when you want, and where you want. With rights and freedom comes responsibility."

RESTRAINING THE CENSORS

In the case of 2 Live Crew, Judge Gonzalez ruled that the group's album crosses the boundary between constitutionally protected speech and obscenity, and for this reason censorship is appropriate. But many people are increasingly concerned about the tendency to resort to censorship as a way of dealing with offensive messages. Across the nation, alarm bells have begun to sound about growing support for censorship. "There is an alarming

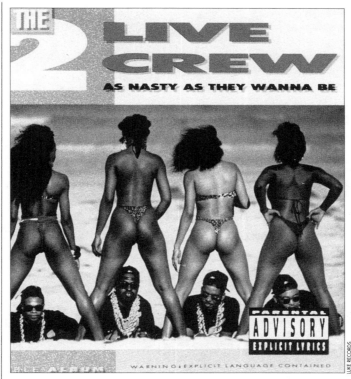

In 1990, Florida District Court Judge Jose Gonzalez declared the lyrics of 2 Live Crew's *As Nasty as They Wanna Be* obscene.

tendency in this country," says Robert Brown, editor of *Editor & Publisher* magazine, "to call for something to be banned if people don't like it. Proliferating pressure groups are proclaiming their view as the 'right' one, and anything to the contrary is unacceptable."

In the San Francisco Bay area, Bobby Lilly, chairman of Californians Against Censorship Together, says that record numbers of people are signing the group's petitions for anti-censorship measures. "I've seen censorship coming like a rising tide for the last three years," says Lilly. "There is a division in this country over what is moral, proper, and ethical. The question is: How much variation, how much choice do you allow?"

For every group that is fighting against

offensive messages, it seems, another is mounting efforts to denounce censorship. One influential organization that has been trying to restrict what it regards as offensive material is the American Family Association, headed by Reverend Donald Wildmon. The AFA, based in Tupelo, Mississippi, has organized pickets at Waldenbooks and other retail booksellers to convince stores to remove *Playboy*, *Penthouse*, and similar magazines from their racks. In April 1990, the 1,300-store Waldenbooks chain replied by running full-page ads in 32 newspapers denouncing "censorship efforts" and "an increasing pattern of intolerance."

Paul Joseph, president of the Florida chapter of the American Civil Liberties Union (ACLU), shares that concern. "We're entering a period of national hysteria over censorship," he says, "a time when it is particularly important for people to understand why speech must be allowed, rather than suppressed."

While some would quarrel with the assertion that American society is gripped with the urge to censor offensive messages, it is indisputably true that free speech — and the limits to acceptable expression — has become a prominent issue on the public agenda. Two hundred years after the passage of the Bill of Rights, the meaning of the First Amendment is being hotly debated.

The First Amendment has the brevity and simplicity of a biblical commandment. It says that "Congress shall make no law . . . abridging the freedom of speech, or of the press." Few words in the Constitution are so familiar, and few are so important. As legal scholar Alexander Meiklejohn once remarked, while most of the Constitution protects the people *from* the government, only the First Amendment ensures the control of the people *over* the government.

Over the past 200 years, the courts have reinterpreted the First Amendment on many occasions. The Supreme Court has extended the protection of the First Amendment to forms of speech that the framers of the Constitution could not have imagined — including rock 'n' roll lyrics, as well as electronic media whose influence is far more pervasive than the newspapers and political pamphlets of the eighteenth century. Yet freedom of speech has never been construed as an absolute right. On one occasion after another, the Supreme Court has taken the position that the right to free speech must be balanced against the community's need to maintain order.

In defense of free speech, Justice Oliver Wendell Holmes, in a minority opinion written in 1919, affirmed the principle at the heart of the First Amendment. "The best test of truth," he wrote, "is the power of thought to get itself accepted in the competition of the market." All ideas, he said, should be allowed to circulate freely in the marketplace of ideas. Because most people will reject bad ideas or harmful messages, he argued, they cannot do much harm.

But Holmes recognized that even a society that places a premium on free expression must limit speech in certain cases. In another case decided in 1919, he wrote that "The most stringent protection of free speech would not protect a man in falsely shouting 'fire' in

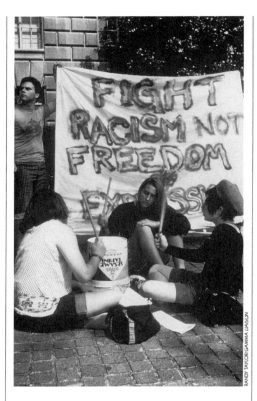

"On campuses across the country, there has been a disturbing upward trend in incidents of hate speech. Many groups have been targeted, including blacks, Asians, Jews, gays, and lesbians."

a theatre and causing panic. . . . The question in every case is whether the words used in such circumstances are of such a nature as to create a clear and present danger that they will bring about substantive evils that Congress has a right to prevent."

So speech is not an absolute right, and all kinds of messages are not protected by the First Amendment. Over the years, the Supreme Court has excluded various forms of expression from the protection of the First Amendment — among them fraudulent advertising, obscenity, and libel.

DELICATE BALANCE

The debate over censorship and free speech requires us to balance the right of free expression against the claims of public morality and the general welfare, and address questions to which people give quite different answers. At what point does free expression — which is occasionally rebellious or outright repulsive — become a threat to the common weal? Which messages pose a social danger, and why? How can we honor a commitment to free speech without doing injury to the other things we value, such as our commitment to diversity and tolerance?

If it is unlikely that a consensus can be reached about which messages are so offensive or socially corrosive that they should be restricted, it becomes increasingly important to address a fundamental question: When confronted with messages that many people find offensive, how should a community respond? Whether the topic is racist epithets, raunchy pop lyrics, or works of art such as the photos of Robert Mapplethorpe, which many people find offensive, the question is how a community should respond and whether

> "There is an alarming tendency in this country to call for something to be banned if people don't like it. Proliferating pressure groups are proclaiming their view as the right one."
>
> — Robert Brown

censorship is appropriate. If official censorship is not appropriate, how *else* can communities respond to offensive messages?

In the case of the rap group 2 Live Crew, for example, the issue is not so much whether their recordings and performances are offensive. Many people agree that they *are*. But what is an appropriate response that is consistent with our commitment to free speech?

In the case of the Madonna video, "Justify My Love," which was banned by MTV in November 1990, the question is whether its depiction of sexual fantasies is appropriate fare for cable television, and whether MTV's decision not to show it unduly restricts viewers' rights to see it.

The same question — how to respond to offensive messages without doing damage to the principle of free speech — is at the center of the controversy over campus speech codes. At Brown University, for example, the expulsion of a 21-year-old junior for shouting racial epithets was praised by some as a strong message about the importance of racial tolerance. Others, however, express concern that vaguely worded speech codes coupled with strong disciplinary actions infringe on the right of students and faculty alike to express unpopular or uncomfortable ideas.

FRAMING THE DEBATE

In this discussion, we will examine the pros and cons of three perspectives on free speech and censorship. The first of these perspectives is the argument for censorship as a response to offensive speech. Certain messages, say advocates of this view, are so dangerous and so destructive to the moral fiber of the community that the laws *must* be used to defend against them.

Those who take a second perspective argue that, while it is inappropriate for *government* to take action to prevent certain messages from being heard, it is entirely appropriate for *private* institutions — such as colleges, TV and radio stations, book publishers — to restrict offensive and potentially damaging messages.

Advocates of a third perspective, who argue for a strict interpretation of the First Amendment, insist that very few forms of expression pose a clear danger to the community. Except for extreme instances such as hard-core child pornography, proponents of this third perspective argue that even the most offensive speech should not be restricted. Bad speech, in this view, calls not for censorship but for moral censure — for efforts to counter that message with cogent criticism.

These three positions frame the debate over freedom of expression. They illustrate the range of views about what kinds of messages are socially corrosive, when it is appropriate to restrict certain messages, and how that should be done. Two hundred years after the Bill of Rights was ratified, it is timely to reexamine the meaning of the First Amendment, to ask how free is *too* free, and which restrictive measures are *too* restrictive in a nation committed to guarding individual rights. ■

CHOICE #1
CLEAR AND PRESENT DANGER: THE CASE FOR LEGAL SANCTIONS

"Words and images that are obscene, hatemongering, or an inducement to violence pose a real danger. Strict limits, backed up with the force of law, are warranted when speech poses a threat to our physical and moral well-being."

Jack Thompson, Susan Brownmiller, and Engedaw Berhanu are three people who have little in common except a shared conviction that certain messages currently protected by the First Amendment pose a clear danger and deserve not only to be condemned but legally restricted.

Thompson is a Florida attorney, an evangelical Christian, and an outspoken critic of obscenity in popular entertainment. By transcribing the lyrics of 2 Live Crew albums, which he dismisses as "sludge" and "toxic waste," and distributing them to law enforcement officials across the state, Thompson became the catalyst for action against *As Nasty as They Wanna Be*.

"It scares me," says Thompson, "that people can advocate the rape of women and get away with it. *As Nasty as They Wanna Be* is such a piece of garbage that it indicts itself. This album isn't about free speech. Its purpose is to titillate and outrage, and glorify the rape of women. These guys are promoting the idea that women are there for nothing but to satisfy men's desires. This stuff makes it more likely that women will be abused."

Thompson, who runs his anti-obscenity campaign from a modest 2-bedroom home in Coral Gables, has recently moved on from

2 Live Crew to protest the music of other rap groups, including Geto Boys and Too Short.

Susan Brownmiller, author of *Against Our Will: Men, Women, and Rape*, shares Thompson's concern about violent messages but comes at it from quite a different perspective. A radical feminist and a liberal, Brownmiller was a founder of a New York-based organization called Women Against Pornography. Her chief concern is the pernicious effects on women of violent pornography.

"I feel surrounded by it," says Brownmiller. "I can't go to the newsstand without being confronted by pictures of women mutilated, tortured, spread into ridiculous postures — pictures designed, I feel, to humiliate my sex and my dignity as a woman. Words and ideas can seduce people, but pictures seduce even more. This is not a question of free speech, but a question of violence."

Engedaw Berhanu is not a well-known figure in Portland, Oregon. But the lawsuit he filed on behalf of the family of Mulugeta Seraw, his nephew, resulted in one of the most prominent court cases in that part of the country in years. Mulugeta Seraw was a young Ethiopian man living in Oregon as a resident alien

KKK marches XX porn X.
slurs satanism bigotry
sexism hazing
Heavy Metal slasher movies
toxic talk
scoping mutilations

DAVID GOTHARD

and would-be college student. In 1988, he was beaten to death with a baseball bat by three young skinheads in a vicious, racially motivated attack.

When the three young men who killed Seraw pleaded guilty to the attack in 1989, they said they were adherents of a group called the White Aryan Resistance, a California-based supremacist organization run by Thomas Metzger, a 53-year-old television repairman and his 23-year-old son, John. No one contended that the Metzgers participated personally in the savage attack or that they helped to single out Seraw as the victim. Rather, the plaintiffs, who asked for more than $10 million in damages, asserted that the Metzgers were negligent in inciting the skinheads to violence. The suit charged that, because the organization's racist messages encouraged the young men to commit violent acts against black people, the Metzgers were liable for the victim's death.

Thomas Metzger contends that the suit is an attempt to silence him and his unpopular message. As the attorney for the Seraw family sees it, however, the Metzgers should be liable for damage that results from their hatemongering words.

SPEECH MATTERS

The common thread in these three individuals' concerns is the conviction that speech matters. In their view, words and images shape attitudes, which in turn shape behavior. Just as good speech can have good effects, bad speech can have bad effects. In the words of Tottie Ellis, vice-president of the Eagle Forum, a conservative, pro-family group, "Words have power in our lives. They make things happen. Words tangibly affect the surroundings into which they are injected." When words and images are obscene, pornographic, profane, violent, or hatemongering, they may cause great harm.

Hatemongers: When speech encourages violence, should it be restricted?

People who share this perspective conclude that official measures must be taken to restrict potentially destructive messages. The Supreme Court has ruled in various obscenity cases that material "utterly without redeeming social value" is not protected by the Constitution. Those who favor this first choice are persuaded that various kinds of messages — obscene lyrics or comedy sketches, messages that threaten the social fabric by encouraging violence, and hateful messages that threaten the commitment to diversity — lack redeeming social value and should be restricted.

As a case in point, consider the lyrics of one of the groups Jack Thompson finds particularly offensive, the Geto Boys. In a track from a 1989 album, "Mind of a Lunatic," the group takes hostility toward women to a gruesome

extreme. The lyric describes a deranged killer of a young woman who slits his victim's throat, and then has sex with the corpse before leaving the scene.

Advocates of this choice are convinced that the only appropriate reaction to such disturbed and disturbing messages is outrage — and public action to prevent their proliferation.

For years, say advocates of the first choice, American society has emphasized individual rights and freedoms, prominently the right to free speech. What we need to recognize, they say, is that many cherished values are in jeopardy because of our reluctance to prohibit particularly offensive messages. As columnist Charles Krauthammer frames the argument: "The call for a pause in the frantic assault on the limits of decency (beyond which lies what used to be taboos) is the expression of a profound disappointment with unrestricted freedom. Many are prepared to make expression a bit less free in order to make their community a bit more whole and wholesome."

Proponents of this choice believe that governmental sanctions are necessary to restrict offensive and dangerous messages — sanctions that include censorship and other measures taken by public agencies such as the Federal Communications Commission and the Justice Department.

"Censorship is not the only answer," says Tottie Ellis, "but it is part of the answer. Those who call for more control are not more righteous. But they do understand that society has the right to prevent or control that which brings about its own destruction."

PERVASIVE AND CORROSIVE

Most people who share this view are concerned about the pervasiveness of corrosive messages that either were not often publicly apparent in the past, or at least did not arrive unbidden in most people's homes. "Twenty years ago," says Tottie Ellis, "pornography was hard to find. Today it is difficult to avoid. There is a flood of X-rated movies and nude centerfolds in magazines that exploit sex. Network television brags about cracking the last taboos, and cable TV channels show explicit sex films. Under the banner of freedom, America is swimming in a sea of filth and violence."

Consider the messages that bombard Americans on a typical day. Violence, murder, and adultery are now routinely portrayed on prime-time television programs. In some communities, messages from hatemongering groups such as the Metzgers' White Aryan Resistance are carried on cable television. Prominent radio personalities specialize in ribald language and ethnic slurs. Magazine stands

2 Live Crew: Mass-marketed filth, or a reflection of a rawer, more culturally diverse reality?

feature row after row of magazines featuring explicit sex. Main Street, in this view, is coming more and more to resemble Times Square.

"It is easy to dismiss protests against pop entertainment and other forms of offensive messages as prudishness," writes *Time* magazine essayist Charles P. Alexander. "To a degree, entertainment reflects what is going on in society. But isn't it possible that pop culture reinforces and amplifies bad behavior? Too much of today's entertainment carries messages that are damaging to young psyches and dangerous to society. Among them: 1) women are sexual objects to be used and abused by men; 2) violence is an effective means of resolving conflicts; 3) it is OK to hate another class of people."

Proponents of this view point to the messages conveyed by some of the most prominent entertainers in the business. Comedian Andrew Dice Clay and his offensive references to women are a prime example. Clay's favorite nursery rhyme begins "Peter, Peter, pumpkin eater / Had a wife, loved to beat her. . . ." and goes downhill from there. In his comedy routines, Clay seems incapable of distinguishing between romantic encounters and date rape. "So I say to the bitch, 'Lose the bra — or I'll cut ya.' Is that a wrong attitude?" Many who hear Clay's routines come away convinced that he is role modeling all the wrong attitudes — and doing

so in sold-out performances. Andrew Dice Clay's routines, say those who share this perspective, are just one manifestation of a tide of offensive messages now washing across American society.

In response to the problem of offensive material, says Charles Alexander, "No one is suggesting that society police every nightclub and root out every raunchy record from store shelves. There will always be filth on the fringes of entertainment. The problem arises when filth becomes mainstream, when it is mass-marketed."

Advocates of official restrictions are convinced that this is just what has happened. Pornography is big business. Dial-a-porn telephone services alone amount to a billion-dollar-a-year business. The success of 2 Live Crew, from this perspective, is a disturbing example of how entertainers who specialize in offensive messages are prospering. By combining the thudding Miami bass sound with rude lyrics, Luther Campbell, the group's leader, has become rich. Campbell owns a Jaguar, a BMW con-

Heavy metal performer Ozzy Osbourne

ULTRAVIOLENCE: MAYHEM GOES MAINSTREAM

If artists, as Ezra Pound said, are "the antennae of the race," they're picking up some bad vibes these days. A few years ago, who would have imagined that one of this season's top-grossing films (Johnathan Demme's *The Silence of the Lambs*) would be about a psychopath who not only murders women but also skins them? Or that meanwhile, over in the world of letters, a young novelist, Bret Easton Ellis, would describe in revolting detail women (and, less notoriously, men, women, children, and dogs) being tortured and butchered? Or that his novel, *American Psycho*, suppressed by its original publisher, boycotted by feminists, and savaged by critics, would become a best-seller? Or that MTV would still be blaring last year's hit song (Aerosmith's "Janie's Got a Gun") about a teen incest victim pumping a bullet into her daddy's brain?

Sure, ultraviolent fare has always been out there — but up until now, it's always been *out there*, on the fringes of mass culture. Nowadays it's the station-wagon set, bumper to bumper at the local Cinema 1-2-3-4-5, that yearns to be titillated by the latest schlocky horror picture show. And the conglomerated, amalgamated media corporations obligingly churn out increasingly vicious movies, books, and records. Mayhem has gone mainstream.

America's addiction to make-believe violence is like any other addiction: it takes more and more to accomplish less and less. Thirty-two people get offed in *RoboCop* (1987). The 1990 sequel serves up 81 corpses. People are upset by the assault of brutal imagery on radio, TV, in the theaters, in best-selling books. It is not any one film or program that is singularly disturbing, it is the appalling accretion of violent entertainment. It is the sense that things have gotten out of control.

There is legitimate alarm at what all this imaginary violence might be contributing to in an increasingly dangerous real life. According to a *Newsweek* poll conducted by The Gallup Organization in mid-March, 40 percent think movie violence is a "very great" cause of the real kind, and an additional 28 percent see it as a "considerable" factor. (Only 11 percent answered "very little.")

Even as we express such heartfelt concerns, we are packing into the multiplexes, lapping up the fictive blood, renting $1.5 billion worth of "action" videos a year, and eagerly awaiting the next Stephen King novel. What kind of people cheer lustily when Bruce Willis pokes an icicle through an eye socket into a baddie's brain? What value is it to

Arnold Schwarzenegger in *The Terminator*

have as talented a writer as Paul Theroux write *Chicago Loop*, about a man who ties up a woman and literally gnaws her to death?

Our fascination with such material is older than Lizzie Borden. What's new is the obsessively detailed description of all 40 whacks, with their attendant shrieks and splatters. Movie violence these days is clearer, louder, more anatomically precise, and a lot sexier. Our ability to feel compassion is brutalized by excessive brutality, especially when it's given that Hollywood sheen.

In all of pop culture (as in most of society), women are the victims of choice. "Consider this a divorce!" Arnold Schwarzenegger bellows just before he blows his wife away in *Total Recall*. An awful lot of hostility against women is being played out in popular culture these days, and it's not pretty.

Playwright Steve Tesich notes, "I have not seen a single anti-rape movie that doesn't promote rape. The very manner in which sexual scenes are shot cause rape to look like an activity that is energizing."

There are those who argue that none of this means much. That no one, except perhaps a lone sicko, listens to the Geto Boys and then jumps the next woman who passes by. That healthy American families don't rush out to buy Uzis just because Schwarzenegger seems so cool wielding one.

But the psychological road between real life and make-believe doesn't run only one way. In this society, mass-produced and mass-consumed movies, books, records, and TV programs are a considerable part of our real lives; they contribute greatly to making us behave the way we do.

Because we are being so inundated with violent images, it is almost impossible to resist growing numb. We risk becoming insensitive to the horror of suffering.

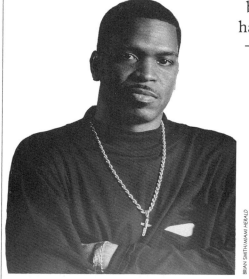

"This is not China or Russia. This is America. We have the right to say what we want to say. We are warranted by the First Amendment to have freedom of expression."
— Luther Campbell, lead singer, 2 Live Crew

vertible, and a Westwind jet. His corporate empire includes three record labels, a recording studio, three discos, and a bulging investment portfolio. One magazine estimates his assets at $11 million. If nothing is done to restrain 2 Live Crew, conclude those who share this perspective, it is all too likely that other entertainers will follow their example.

In the *Miller* decision, Chief Justice Warren Burger warned against misinterpreting the First Amendment: "To equate the free and robust exchange of ideas and political debate with commercial exploitation of obscene materials," he wrote, "demeans the grand conception of the First Amendment and its high purpose."

PROTECTION AGAINST HARM

Advocates of official restrictions point out that government regulates and prohibits many things deemed dangerous to the public or hazardous to our health. When it is determined that certain products are harmful — asbestos, for example, or a drug such as thalidomide — people call for government-imposed restrictions. Yet, say proponents of the first choice, corrosive messages are spreading like wildfire, protected by the cloak of the First Amendment.

Columnist George Will puts the argument clearly: "America today is capable of terrific intolerance about smoking or toxic waste that threatens trout. We legislate against smoking in restaurants. Yet singing 'Me So Horny' is a constitutional right. Secondary smoke is carcinogenic; celebration of torn vaginas is 'mere words.' Only a deeply confused society is more concerned about protecting lungs than minds, trout than black women."

Concern about the coarsening effects of exposure to toxic measures is widely shared. Reporter Juan Williams of the *Washington Post,* for example, is an outspoken critic of 2 Live Crew. Williams, a black man, is especially concerned about the group's impact on the black community. 2 Live Crew, he says, "is selling corruption — self-hate — to vulnerable young minds in a weak black America." The issue, says Williams, is the abuse of women, particularly black women. The unfortunate effect of the Crew's crude message, in his view, is

"As Nasty as They Wanna Be isn't about free speech. Its purpose is to titillate and outrage, and glorify rape. It scares me that people can advocate rape and get away with it."
— Jack Thompson, Florida attorney, leader of the effort to have 2 Live Crew's album declared obscene

the corruption of the sensibilities of young blacks. Lyrics of such groups as 2 Live Crew, says Williams, distort their conception of "good sex, good relationships, and good times."

While many of the people who favor restricting offensive expression are conservatives, Susan Brownmiller insists that liberals should be equally concerned. "Pornography is propaganda against women, and a powerful spur to action. It functions quite similarly to anti-Semitic or racist propaganda. It promotes a climate of opinion in which sexual hostility against women is not only tolerated but encouraged. It's dangerous and it incites people to commit violent acts."

However, says Brownmiller, "the same liberals who have come to understand that 'nigger' jokes and portrayals of shuffling, rolling-eyed servants perpetuate the degrading myth of black inferiority fervidly maintain that pornographic materials quaintly called 'adult' or 'erotic' books and movies must be preserved as a constitutional right.

"The anti-pornography movement,"

> "Many are prepared to make expression a bit less free in order to make their community a bit more whole and wholesome."
>
> — Charles Krauthammer

Brownmiller concludes, "must convince people that they can be good liberals, support the First Amendment, have a terrific sex life — and oppose pornography and fight to curtail it."

EVIDENCE OF DANGER

Recalling Justice Holmes's "clear and present danger" criterion, people who hold this view argue that, since certain kinds of messages encourage violent crime and pose a threat to the nation's moral well-being, such speech must be restrained. "If our commitment to First Amendment values demands the toleration of some sexually explicit materials," writes Donald Downs, a professor of political science at the University of Wisconsin, "society is still entitled to protect itself from clear and specific harms."

The harm, in this view, need not be as palpable as the danger posed by a person who shouts "fire" in a crowded theatre. The Supreme Court has ruled that "the interest of the public in the quality of life, the total community environment . . . and the public safety itself" are legitimate reasons for restraint.

Those who take this perspective are convinced that certain messages pose a real danger, and cite studies to support their view. Various investigations show that exposure to violent pornography tends to desensitize men to sexual violence and increase the inclination to engage in aggression toward women.

For example, research conducted by social psychologist Edward Donnerstein suggests that "exposure to even a few minutes of sexually violent pornography, such as scenes of rape and other forms of sexual violence against women, can lead to anti-social attitudes and behavior." Donnerstein says that exposure increases the likelihood that the viewer will accept the myth that women want to be raped. It increases the likelihood of a man saying that he

would commit a rape. It also demonstrably increases aggressive behavior against women in a laboratory setting. And it decreases sensitivity to the plight of the rape victim. "If brief exposure to sexually violent pornography can have these effects," asks Donnerstein, "what are the effects of exposure to hours of such material?"

Other researchers have found a correlation between the availability of pornography and the incidence of sex crimes in particular communities. In addition to laboratory studies, say proponents of this choice, there is a statistical link between the increase in rape and the availability of pornography. Police reports often link pornography to the commission of sex crimes. Since 1960, the incidence of rape in the United States has increased at an alarming rate. The rate of forcible rape doubled between 1960 and 1970, then doubled again in the 1970s, and it has continued to rise since the early 1980s. It is no coincidence, say proponents of this view, that this has happened at the same

time that violent pornography has become more readily available.

In the words of former Surgeon General C. Everett Koop, "I am certain that pornography that portrays sexual aggression as pleasurable for the victim is at the root of much of the rape that occurs today. Impressionable men — many of them still adolescents — see this material and get the impression that women like to be hurt, to be humiliated, to be forced to do things that they do not want to do. It is a false and vicious stereotype."

Proponents of this choice are equally concerned about the effects of repeated exposure to non-sexual violence. The average American, according to the National Coalition on Television Violence, views eight to ten hours of violent programming per week. "Because of TV," says James Alan Fox, a Northeastern University researcher, "we've become quite used to murder. By repetition, the viewer becomes desensitized to it. It's less of a taboo. In a sense, prime time has unleashed a permit for murder."

Several years ago, University of Illinois psychologists Leonard Eron and

L. Rowell Huesmann studied the effects of violent TV fare on children who watch it. They found that 8-year-old children who watched significant amounts of violent TV programs were more likely as 30-year-old adults to commit violent crimes and to engage in child or spouse abuse. In the investigators' words: "We believe that heavy exposure to televised violence is one of the causes of aggressive behavior, crime, and violence in society."

MORAL INFLUENCE

Those who would impose additional restrictions on certain kinds of messages are equally concerned about their impact on public morality. In the words of James Underwood, "Social orders are established and laws passed to protect people against the sordid influences that demean life and are every bit as harmful as a blow to the head."

In different ways, say proponents of public restrictions, both pornography and hatemongering messages are morally harmful and should be restricted. This was the message conveyed by the authors of the minority report of the 1970 Presidential Commission on Obscenity and Pornography: "Society has a legitimate concern in maintaining moral standards. It follows logically that government has a legitimate interest in attempting to protect such standards against any source which threatens them. We believe that government must legislate to regulate pornography in order to protect the social interest in order and morality."

The same logic leads to the conclusion that hatemongering messages must be restricted. Such messages, say advocates of official restrictions, pose a clear danger to minority groups. Recent statistics show an upward trend in violence directed against various minorities. For example, according to a study released early in 1991 by the National Gay and

Lesbian Task Force, violence aimed at gay men and lesbians rose by more than 40 percent in 1990 in 6 cities where such incidents were monitored.

Especially at a time when hatred against minorities is on the rise, say advocates of this choice, official action must be taken to keep hatemongering groups from spreading their divisive message. Those who argue for official restraints on hateful messages insist that all views and opinions are *not* the same. Messages such as the Metzgers' cable TV show "Race and Reason" are a threat to free expression, not a manifestation of it. The apparent intent of the show, which consists largely of taunts and insults from white supremacists, is to intimidate. In this case, say advocates of restrictions, since the show's message is intolerant, censoring it would not undermine free speech. In fact, by keeping an intimidating message from being heard, censorship in this case would permit *freer* expression.

WHAT CAN BE DONE

Official actions of various kinds have been taken to restrict corrosive messages. Advocates of this choice favor the action taken in July 1988, in Kansas City, Missouri, to prevent the Ku Klux Klan from using the public access cable TV channel to disseminate its racist message. In that case, the city council voted to eliminate the city's public access cable TV channel rather than permitting a program produced by the Klan. (A year later, when faced with a lawsuit claiming that the city's elimination of public access violated the right to free speech, the city council reversed its decision.)

It is in the area of pornography that advocates of restriction have been most specific. Actions that have been proposed or taken in Memphis and Minneapolis illustrate the kinds of official actions that can be taken.

In April 1990, the Memphis City Council signed an ordinance — the most far-reaching law of its kind in the United States — that holds performers and producers of live entertainment shows liable for anything harmful that minors see or hear at such events. The stringent ordinance bans minors from performances involving "nudity, sexual excitement, sexual conduct, excess violence or sadomasochistic abuse." The ordinance specifies fines not only for producers and performers, but also for parents who knowingly allow minors to attend them.

Florence Leffler, a Memphis City Council member who voted for the proposal, says she believes offensive lyrics are contributing to the deterioration of American society. "I'll do everything I can to try to protect the minds of young

> "Censorship is not the only answer, but it is part of the answer. Those who call for more control understand that society has the right to prevent or control that which brings about its own destruction."
>
> — Tottie Ellis

people from that kind of garbage," she says. "If you're a parent and your value system is . . . sick, then I'm going to try to protect your 12-year-old from you."

As of early 1991, no arrests had been made under the provisions of the new ordinance. But according to Beth Wade, managing director of the Mid-South Coliseum, some bands now clean up their act when they come to Memphis. Comedian Andrew Dice Clay passed up Memphis entirely on a recent national tour when he failed to receive assurances that he would not be arrested.

In Minneapolis, a different kind of proposal has been put forward to curtail pornography. Janella Miller, an attorney formerly with the Pornography Resource Center in Minneapolis, is a prominent supporter of a legislative measure first put forward in Minneapolis that goes beyond existing obscenity laws and offers a new way to prosecute individuals who produce pornography. The statute (which became law in the mid-1980s in Indianapolis and was subsequently struck down by the Federal Appeals Court) was drafted by feminist writer Andrea Dworkin and University of Minnesota law professor Catherine MacKinnon.

Unlike censorship, which implies official examination of lyrics, plays, or pictures for the purpose of suppressing what is objectionable, this ordinance works in a different way. It provides no mechanism for telling people what messages cannot be published or broadcast. Rather, it is based on the assertion that, by exercising their First Amendment rights to free expression, pornographers deprive women of their civil liberties. By defining pornography as a form of sex discrimination and as a violation of women's rights, the ordinance sends a message to pornographers. If they disseminate messages that lead to harm or discrimination against women, they can be held legally responsible.

In its overall intent, the ordinance is similar to the suit brought against Thomas Metzger and his son in Oregon by the family of the young man who was beaten to death by adherents of the Metzgers' racist organization. The point of that suit and the proposed anti-pornography ordinance is that those who disseminate messages that have harmful consequences should be held legally responsible for the damage they cause.

"If the ordinance were applied," writes Janella Miller, "pornographers would undoubtedly choose not to publish certain materials because it would be too costly to defend themselves. Consequently, there would be fewer pornographic pictures, movies, and books. The harm done to women by pornography is great enough to justify limitations on the pornographers' right to freedom of speech."

People who hold this view do not necessarily agree about what kinds of speech are so harmful as to justify official restrictions. Some, for example, are not particularly concerned about offensive lyrics or comedy routines, but

they would like to see sexually explicit material taken off the magazine racks. Others are not particularly concerned about those kinds of messages, but they are deeply disturbed by hatemongering messages of groups such as the White Aryan Resistance.

What they agree on is that strict limits on freedom of expression — backed up with the force of law — are warranted whenever speech represents a clear danger to our physical or moral well-being. As important as freedom of expression is, it is not the *only* thing we value. For this reason, the power of the law must be used to restrict certain kinds of messages.

As Midge Decter, executive director of the Committee for the Free World, points out, our reluctance to draw the line and to forbid corrosive messages is a troubling symptom of moral uncertainty. "We have reached a point of extreme confusion in this society. We no longer have any idea what our values are. If the law cannot involve an assertion of community standards, what is it for? And if we have no community standards in these areas, we are already more than halfway to the abyss. We cannot legislate attitudes. But, as a society, we must do something to protect ourselves."

WHAT CRITICS SAY

While critics of this position acknowledge the existence of a lot of verbal sludge, they differ about the extent of the problem and whether it is advisable to deal with it by invoking legal sanctions.

As critics see it, claims of a "tidal wave" of offensive messages are a gross exaggeration. While controversial performers such as 2 Live Crew and Andrew Dice Clay get the lion's share of media attention, their acts are by no means typical. Critics contend that bluenosed advocates of official restrictions make the mistake of taking today's entertainers more seriously than the performers do themselves. As Richard Corliss comments, "Clay and most of the other new raunch artists don't believe for a moment what they're saying. Metal musicians are not serious satanists; their concerts are just theatre pieces — *Cats* with a nasty yowl. Clay is not the pathetic strutting stud he seems on stage; that's just a character. (Was Jack Benny really stingy? Is Pee-wee Herman really a goony child?) Clay and the other entertainers on the edge are playing out fantasies — their own and their audience's — of the baddest boy in school, of the kid your parents prayed to God you would never become."

In their raunchier moments, critics of the first choice argue, entertainers such as 2 Live Crew reflect a rawer and more culturally diverse reality — a reality some advocates of official censorship would like to deny. "Like them or not," says Corliss, "today's blue comics and shock rockers know what is happening. That is why they are popular. Get used to it, America: we live in a four-letter world."

MARGULIES
©1985 HOUSTON POST
United Feature Syndicate

United Features Syndicate, Inc.

The call for censorship, say critics, is also based on a misunderstanding of the problem. Most critics of this position agree that violence is a pervasive problem in American society. But, says writer Robert Shea, "The notion that pornography causes sex crime is magical thinking, on a par with the medieval belief that witches cause plagues. Fighting pornography may give people the feeling that they are doing something about the frightful problem of sexual crime, just as reinstating capital punishment gives them the feeling that they are doing something about murder. In both instances, the sense of accomplishment is illusory."

As critics see it, advocates of this choice misunderstand the connection between what people see — on film and TV, in books, and magazines — and what they do. Ideas and images certainly influence behavior. But to assert a cause-and-effect relationship oversimplifies the complex connection between images, fantasies, and behavior.

"What the censors are offering," says writer David Rieff, "is nothing more than the old American fantasy of prohibition. Ban alcohol, and no one will drink; ban racist speech, and no one will be a racist; ban pornography, and no one will ever have a perverse thought again."

Critics of legal sanctions point out that the evidence of studies on the effect of exposure to pornographic material is far from conclusive. A 1985 report from a commission that examined the topic for the Canadian government stated that social science research on the effects of pornography is so contradictory and chaotic that no firm conclusion is possible.

After years of studies on the topic, reports Robert Shea, "we still have no proof that pornography, even the violent sort, causes sex crime. We have only studies showing that, in a laboratory setting, for a brief period, men who see erotic-violent films will act more aggressively toward women when permitted to do so by an authority figure."

> "What the censors are offering is nothing more than the old fantasy of prohibition. Ban racist speech, and no one will be a racist; ban pornography, and no one will ever have a perverse thought again."
>
> — David Rieff

THE PUBLIC INTEREST

A serious problem with the argument for official restrictions, say critics, is that it doesn't acknowledge the danger of resorting to censorship. Since obscenity is so hard to define, efforts to restrict it — such as the Memphis ordinance about public performances — hinge on vague terms that permit public officials a great deal of latitude for personal interpretation. Justice Potter Stewart once defended his ability to identify pornography by saying "I know it when I see it" — but so did officials at the U.S. Customs Bureau who kept Joyce's *Ulysses,* one of the literary masterpieces of the twentieth century, from being distributed in the United States for 11 years.

What is troubling, say critics, is that the moral crusaders who propose to ban certain messages are rarely willing to stop at the most offensive cases. "Once we begin selectively defining which words are acceptable," says Florida Republican Senator Connie Mack, "we enter a slippery slope where freedom is compromised."

Critics are concerned, for example, about the precedent established by a January 1991 Federal District Court ruling in Florida that the display of scantily clad women in pinup calendars in the workplace amounts to sexual harassment. Women's rights advocates hailed the decision, saying it should prompt employers to remove such pictures from the workplace. In his ruling, Judge Howell Melton found that the presence of such pinups amounts to harassment, a "visual assault on the sensibilities of female workers." But critics of the decision worry about workers' rights to privacy and free expression, and about what *else* might be regarded as an assault on the sensibilities of female workers.

To illustrate what can happen when legislators begin to regard certain words as unacceptable, critics note that in February 1991 the Colorado House of Representatives passed a bill prohibiting disparaging comments about perishable fruit, vegetables, and dairy products. Recalling the 1989 controversy over Alarsprayed apples and how it hurt apple growers, the bill's supporters insisted that agricultural products should be protected from defamatory comments.

To free-speech advocates, this episode is a revealing example of a serious problem. Once laws are passed to prevent malicious comments, they say, it appears sensible — even compelling — to extend the same protection in other areas where speech might cause harm. Eventually, this leads to a situation in which many messages are prohibited on the grounds that they are disparaging, and we are free to say very little.

Official sanctions against offensive messages have another corrosive effect, say critics. They intimidate people to the point of self-censorship. Over the past few years, the Federal Communications Commission has cracked down on radio and TV stations that broadcast offensive material. Even though the courts have upheld only one FCC fine for indecency since 1987, the FCC's aggressive actions have apparently had a chilling effect on the broadcasting industry. In the words of attorney Timothy Dyk, "Broadcasters have been saying to themselves, 'When in doubt, leave it out,' and there are large areas of doubt. Even if material has serious merit — plays, films, or even dance — it may be found to be indecent. The effect has been self-censorship, because no one wants to be fined by the FCC."

19

WHY CENSORSHIP DOESN'T WORK

Accordingly, critics of this position oppose such measures as the Memphis ordinance and the statute passed in Indianapolis that defines pornography as a form of sex discrimination.

"Anti-pornography ordinances do more harm than good for women," in the words of a report from the Feminist Anti-Censorship Taskforce. "Removing sexually explicit materials would not stop violence against women. Such ordinances would give enormous power to the courts to interpret and rule on a wide variety of sexual images. These laws could be used to attack and limit feminist self-expression. This ordinance attempts to enforce, with the power of the state, one view of pornography. But many feminists believe that the law represents a dangerous and misguided strategy."

Novelist Erica Jong adds that "We should be wary of imposing laws, such as the Indianapolis ordinance, which allow the 'victims' of pornography to sue for damages. Our society is already obsessed with lawsuits and litigation. We cannot legislate these attitudes out of existence. Instead, we must seek to change the hearts and minds of people."

Those who criticize Memphis' stringent law that holds performers liable for what minors see or hear in live performances do so on similar grounds. Soon after the ordinance was passed in April 1990, the ACLU filed suit on behalf of a Memphis father, charging that the law deprives parents of the right to control the performances their children may attend.

"In my opinion," says Larry McDaniel, a former Air Force sergeant and one of the plaintiffs, "they're taking away my rights as a parent. That's what ticks me off. These people don't send my kids to school or pay my bills, and yet they turn around and tell my children what concerts they can and cannot go to."

Critics of censorship agree. It is the parent's responsibility to monitor what their children see and do — theirs and nobody else's.

As critics of official restrictions see it, even hatemongers such as the White Aryan Resistance should not be muzzled. As tragic as the brutal beating of

Art students in Cincinnati protesting efforts to censor an exhibit by photographer Robert Mapplethorpe.

the young Ethiopian in Oregon was, the best way to prevent such situations is not to silence those who spread hateful messages.

From this perspective, it was a mistake for the Kansas City Council to decide to eliminate its public access channel rather than running a program produced by the Ku Klux Klan. In a lawsuit filed to force the city council to reverse its decision — which succeeded in convincing the council to restore the channel — the ACLU declared that, "It is easy to support a public forum when the message carried over it is in the

mainstream. It is not so easy, for most people, when the message is hateful and wrongheaded. But public access programming is a public forum, the electronic equivalent of a soapbox. It is no different from a public park or street available for political speeches and demonstrations."

Similarly, it would be wrong, said a spokesman for the ACLU in Oregon, to punish the Metzgers on the grounds that their speech unintentionally caused a death. Advocacy of ideas — however offensive — is protected by the First Amendment. "The Supreme Court has said quite clearly that only intentional incitement of imminent racial violence does not deserve the protection of the First Amendment," said Michael H. Simon, a Portland attorney who helped draft the ACLU brief.

The main point of the First Amendment, say critics of official censorship, is that all views may be heard. Bad messages can be countered or rebutted — but they should not be censored. As the Supreme Court declared in the *Roth* decision, "All ideas having even the slightest redeeming social importance — unorthodox ideas, controversial ideas, even ideas hateful to the prevailing climate of opinion — have the full protection of the guaranties, unless excludable because they encroach on the limited area of more important interests."

Imposing official restrictions is not the best way to deal with offensive speech, conclude critics. In the words of Richard Corliss, "You may despise the work of Clay, or Mapplethorpe, or 2 Live Crew, and still embrace the concept of an America that allows them to find or lose an audience. They have the right to offend. You have the right to be offended. That is still the American way." ■

CHOICE #2
SELF-IMPOSED RESTRICTIONS:
THE PRIVATE-SECTOR SOLUTION

"While government censorship is ill advised, sensible limits should be enforced by private institutions. Publishers, radio and TV stations, college campuses, and other institutions should restrict offensive speech when it violates community standards."

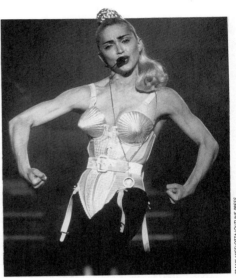

Madonna controversy: "Justify My Love," said MTV, was too hot to handle.

While some people favor public measures as the best way to restrict offensive messages, others who are equally concerned about corrosive speech favor a different remedy. Government should not prevent potentially offensive messages from being heard, say advocates of a second perspective. But it is perfectly appropriate for private-sector gatekeepers — such as disc jockeys, radio and TV stations, publishers, and club owners — to exercise judgment about what they will broadcast or publish.

Until a few years ago, racist, sexist, or anti-gay remarks or messages were generally shrugged off as merely rude or in bad taste. Today, such expressions are often met with reprisals. A series of recent, widely publicized incidents suggests that media executives are ready to draw the line when faced with words or images that are tasteless and offensive.

In 1990, for example, TV commentator Andy Rooney was temporarily removed from his post on "60 Minutes" after he was quoted as saying that blacks have "watered down their genes because the less intelligent ones . . . have the most children" — a remark Rooney denies having made. The alleged remark was made public by a magazine that had expressed concern about an earlier Rooney remark — for which he apologized — that homosexual sex is one of several largely preventable causes of death.

When David Burke, then president of the CBS News Division, sent Rooney to the woodshed, he issued a stern announcement: "CBS News cannot tolerate such remarks, or anything that approximates such comments, since they in no way reflect the views of this organization." Soon after, the *New York Times* editorial page praised the move: "Score 10 on the commonsense scale for David Burke . . . for his handling of the newest outbreak of slighting words."

Top-40 radio stations acted in a similar fashion in 1987 when pop singer George Michael released his steamy single, "I Want Your Sex." Concerned that the lyrics condoned casual sex at a time when AIDS and other sexual diseases were rampant, station managers in a dozen cities decided not to air the record. They were widely praised for their decision. In the words of a *USA Today* editorial: "Broadcasters have the right to exercise discretion. It's wise for stations to yank records that offend their listeners." MTV joined the protest against "I Want Your Sex" by returning the video to Columbia Records with a complaint about "unacceptable visuals."

In November 1990, MTV was in the news again for drawing the line about another video it considered offensive, Madonna's "Justify My Love." The video, which Madonna says illustrates her erotic fantasies, is a catalog of sexual practices that many people find offensive. MTV said it was too hot to handle. "We respect her work as an artist and we think she makes great videos," said MTV executives in a prepared statement. "This one is just not for us."

PARENTAL ADVISORY:
THE LABELING CONTROVERSY

On September 19, 1985, spokespersons for a newly formed group called the Parents' Music Resource Center (PMRC) appeared before the Senate Committee on Commerce, Science, and Transportation to focus public attention on the proliferation of raunch in popular music. Led by Tipper Gore, wife of Senator Albert Gore, Jr., the PMRC has been influential in calling attention to the problem.

Because offensive lyrics can have an insidious effect on impressionable minors, says Tipper Gore, they should be restricted. The goal of the PMRC, however, is not official censorship. Rather, the group's goal has been to persuade the record industry to agree to a voluntary labeling system, under which a parental advisory sticker would be attached to recordings containing offensive lyrics.

Although many in the music industry feel that labeling systems are cumbersome and restrictive, the Recording Industry Association of America (RIAA) — the trade group whose members produce 90 percent of the musical recordings released in the U.S. — agreed in 1985 to label some records, cassettes, and compact discs. The RIAA's decision was made, in large part, as a response to the PMRC's concerns.

But, according to the PMRC, the voluntary labeling agreement that was in effect from 1986 to 1990 proved ineffective because labels were applied inconsistently

Spurred, in part, by the controversy that followed the release of 2 Live Crew's *As Nasty as They Wanna Be*, more than a dozen state legislatures began debating bills in 1990 that would mandate warning stickers on offensive albums. A Missouri bill that served as model legislation in other states called for a fluorescent yellow sticker with the following text: "Warning: May contain explicit lyrics descriptive of or advocating one or more of the following: nudity, satanism, suicide, sodomy, incest, bestiality, sadomasochism, adultery, murder, morbid violence, or deviant sexual conduct in a violent context, or the illegal use of drugs or alcohol. Parental advisory." The bill also set age restrictions that would prohibit minors from purchasing offensive recordings, and defined legal sanctions for retailers who violate the restrictions.

Most musicians and executives in the recording industry feel that such laws would have a chilling effect on recording artists. "Won't retailers, in fear of fines and jail, stick those labels on any recording that might conceivably fit those broadly state-defined categories?" asks columnist Tom Wicker. "Won't some artists be influenced to alter their creative works to avoid labeling and the resulting damage to sales? And if a state can ban, or require retailers to label a commercial recording, why can't it require booksellers to label books, since many may contain words or ideas as explicit as any rap lyric?"

To head off legislative measures and mandatory labeling, the RIAA announced a new voluntary labeling policy in March 1990. The association agreed that record producers would place a sticker — with uniform design, wording, and placement — on offensive recordings. The label reads, "Explicit Lyrics — Parental Advisory," and is intended to be instantly recognizable to consumers. According to the new RIAA procedure, the decision about which recordings carry the sticker will be left to individual artists and musicians.

— *Bill Carr*

Simon and Schuster, one of the largest American publishing firms, made a similar decision in 1990 when it decided not to publish a manuscript for which it had paid a $300,000 advance to author Bret Easton Ellis. The book, *American Psycho* — which graphically depicts a serial killer who murders and dismembers women, children, and animals — was described by the president of the Los Angeles chapter of the National Organization for Women as "a how-to novel on the torture and dismemberment of women." Acknowledging the firm's responsibilities to exercise editorial judgment about what it publishes, Simon and Schuster's president, Richard Snyder, said the decision not to publish the manuscript was based on "a matter of taste."

INDUSTRY STANDARDS

Advocates of private-sector restrictions agree that America is suffering from a wave of crude and caustic messages — pornographic, violent, and hatemongering. "No society can survive if the only rule is 'anything goes,'" writes essayist Charles Alexander. "So the question becomes 'What goes?' In general, this question should be answered not by government but by artists, producers, theatre owners, and media executives."

The virtue of the private-sector solution, say advocates of this choice, is that it doesn't put the authority of the laws — or of law enforcement officials — behind any particular rules about what can be said publicly and what cannot be said. The best way to reflect community standards, in this view, is to allow private institutions to decide on a case-by-case basis what violates local standards. Advocates of the private-sector solution are convinced this is the most prudent way to balance concern for community standards with a commitment to pluralism.

> "In general, the question 'What goes?' should be answered not by government but by artists, producers, theater owners, and media executives."
>
> — Charles Alexander

Advocates of this choice note another reason for private-sector restrictions. It is one thing for Andy Rooney or George Michael or Madonna to say what they want as private citizens. It is another matter entirely for CBS or MTV to determine what messages are consistent with their corporate responsibility and the audiences they serve. Private institutions have a right and a duty, from this perspective, to define limits to the kinds of speech they will permit. CBS, MTV, and Brown University establish and enforce codes appropriate to themselves as freestanding, private institutions with a specific commitment to the public. From this second perspective, that is why Brown University, or Stanford, or other universities (and not the U.S. court system) should oversee speech on campus; and it is why MTV (but not the courts) should decide which recordings it will air, and which recordings are offensive to its audience.

As illustrated by the way the entertainment industry modified its message about drugs, the private-sector solution is often effective, say advocates of this choice. In the 1960s and 1970s, the entertainment industry — from the Beatles to *Easy Rider* — generally portrayed drug use as glamorous and socially acceptable. But in the 1980s, as the perils of drug use became more apparent, the entertainment industry changed its message. In recent years, by presenting a strong and consistent message that drugs are dangerous, the media have played an important role in changing American attitudes and drug-related behavior.

It is wrong, say proponents of this second course of action, to assume that every serious problem requires government action. Censorship and other kinds of official restrictions are too blunt a tool to use to stem the tide of offensive messages. That was Louisiana Governor

Andy Rooney: Removed from his "60 Minutes" post because of offensive remarks

Buddy Roemer's point in a July 1990 press conference in which he announced his veto of a record-labeling bill. In the Louisiana legislature, as in 18 other states, legislative proposals have been put forward to require warning labels on recordings dealing with such topics as drugs, incest, murder, and suicide. The Louisiana bill would have required warning labels on recordings about such matters as deviant sex, violence, bigotry, and drug abuse, and it would have banned the sale of such records to minors.

At the press conference where he announced his veto, Governor Roemer said he agreed about the need to inform parents of the content of recordings. But he disagreed with the idea that passing a law is the best way to deal with the problem. In his words, "Trash lyrics containing references to suicide, sex, drugs, rape, and incest are potentially harmful to impressionable youth." But he said that the best way to deal with

the problem is for the recording industry to police itself by attaching a "parental advisory" sticker on offensive recordings.

"In a free America, where speech is constitutionally protected," said Roemer, "the best method of informing the public is through voluntary compliance with industry standards, similar to what the movie industry has done successfully."

Standing next to Roemer at the press conference, Jay Berman, president of the Recording Industry Association of America, endorsed the veto. The governor's veto, said Berman, "sends a clear message that the voluntary labeling system and artistic freedom can coexist without government intervention."

CAMPUS CODES

Among private-sector efforts to restrict offensive speech, speech codes that have recently been instituted on more than 125 American campuses provide the clearest example of the measures private institutions are taking to resist offensive and hateful messages.

Many of today's college students, writes Phillip Weiss in a recent account of abuses that gave rise to campus codes at Dartmouth College, "do not want to sort out the issues among themselves. Nor do they want to go to the D.A. They're evidently comfortable with *in loco parentis*, the college's traditional power as substitute parent." The premise of efforts to institute campus speech codes, says Weiss, is that abusive language "is a problem not for society at large to solve but for the campus family, with its own special code of behavior."

Speech codes, which didn't exist until a few years ago on most campuses, are a response to a rash of racist, derogatory, and demeaning comments. Incidents of bias-motivated harassment, one of the most disturbing developments in American higher education in years, have been reported on many campuses. In 1990, People for the American Way, a nonprofit group based in Washington, D.C., surveyed 128 institutions of higher learning to gauge the extent of the problem. On roughly 60 percent of the campuses surveyed, incidents of intolerance on campus had been reported over the previous 18 months. Fifty-seven percent of the colleges and universities acknowledged that intolerance is a significant problem.

At the University of Michigan, which was one of the first institutions to try to deal with the problem, someone distributed fliers on campus in January 1987 declaring "open season" on blacks, referring to them as "saucer lips, porch monkeys, and jigaboos." Soon after, the student radio station broadcast racially offensive jokes, which brought to a head concern about racial harassment.

At Dartmouth College in October 1990, the *Dartmouth Review*, a politically conservative student weekly, touched off campus protests by printing anti-Semitic passages from Hitler's *Mein Kampf*. "I believe today that I am acting in the sense of the Almighty Creator," the *Review* said in its credo under the masthead, quoting from *Mein Kampf*. "By warding off the Jews, I am fighting for the Lord's work."

On other campuses, there have been reports of Native American students being heckled and taunted during an annual campus powwow, of gay students being publicly denounced as "faggots," and of fraternities electing a "Jewish-American Princess" to mock and degrade.

In the words of a report from People for the American Way, "Evidence of strain and divisiveness is everywhere — from overt acts of bigotry to an increasingly acrimonious debate over the con-

Dear Mom and Dad,
Being in collidge is easier then I thought and it's fun too. Yestidoy me and some guys burned a cross in front of a black kid's dorm and the night before we beat up a Jewish kid and painted a swastika on his locker. Tomorrow we're going to trash one of them smart aleck Asians. A chip off the old block, eh?
That's all for now.
Love, Merwin

P.S. I could use some more money.

DON WRIGHT/THE PALM BEACH POST

tent and ideology of course curricula. Headlines and scattered reports fail to do justice to the full significance of campus conflict." Sociologist Howard Ehrlich, research director at the National Institute Against Prejudice and Violence, estimates that some 20-25 percent of all minority students on campus are victimized annually.

Such incidents, says Mary Ellen Gale, professor at Whittier School of Law in California, "exemplify the moral degeneration of public values in the past decade and the resurgence of racism, homophobia, and religious prejudice."

Whether the issue is racist, sexist, or anti-gay messages on campus, proponents of campus speech codes insist that harassment must be taken seriously. To protect and promote diversity, say advocates of campus sanctions, rules must be clearly spelled out about what kinds of speech will not be tolerated.

REASONS FOR HARSH MEASURES

Serious sanctions against hate speech are justified, say advocates of campus speech codes, because the harm inflicted by racial speech is real and long-lasting. "Psychic injury is no less an injury," says Charles Lawrence, law professor at Stanford Univer-

sity, "than being struck in the face, and often is far more severe. Racial epithets and harassment often cause deep emotional scarring, and feelings of anxiety and fear that pervade every aspect of a victim's life. Victims of hate propaganda have experienced physiological symptoms and emotional stress ranging from rapid pulse rate and difficulty in breathing to nightmares, post-traumatic stress disorder, psychosis, and suicide.

"Face-to-face racial insults, like fighting words, are undeserving of First Amendment protection," says Lawrence. "The experience of being called 'nigger,' 'spic,' 'Jap,' or 'kike' is like receiving a slap in the face." Assaultive racist speech functions as a preemptive strike. The racial invective is experienced as a blow, not a proffered idea, and, once the blow is struck, it is unlikely that a dialogue will follow.

On various campuses, there are reports of minority students who, as a result of verbal harassment, have left college or fled to other campuses where their own minority predominates. Others choose to stay, but adjust their conduct to avoid future harassment. In either case, say advocates of strict

> "We're trying to discourage people from browbeating others who simply may be different. Racists shouldn't be able to abuse minorities."
>
> — Thomasiana Clemons

speech codes, such verbal harassment is an unacceptable affront and a denial of equal educational opportunity. "When victims of hate speech relinquish the opportunity they once sought to confront and challenge new ideas and to communicate with people of different backgrounds and viewpoints," says Mary Ellen Gale, "both they and their perpetrators suffer the kinds of losses the First Amendment seems designed to prevent."

Since harassing speech also denies the victim's Fourteenth Amendment rights to an equal education, concludes Mary Ellen Gale, "harassment may be prohibited and punished — even when it consists just of words."

PROHIBITING HARASSMENT

In an effort to curb racial incidents and discriminatory harassment, more than 100 universities have adopted speech codes or amended student conduct codes to restrict forms of expression that are considered offensive. In the words of Thomasiana Clemons, director of affirmative action at the University of Connecticut, "We're trying to discourage people from browbeating others who simply may be different. Racists shouldn't be able to abuse minorities." The sanctions for infractions range from written warnings to mandatory counseling and expulsion.

Campus codes generally correspond to one of three models. Some policies, such as those at the University of Connecticut and at Stanford University, ban speech that amounts to "fighting words." As the Supreme Court justices put it in a 1942 decision, restrictions on speech are justified when it is "likely to provoke the average person to retaliate and thereby cause a breach of the peace."

A code proposed by Stanford's Student Conduct Legislative Council, for example, would have prohibited face-to-face attacks characterized by "obscenities, epithets, and other forms of expression that by accepted community stan-dards degrade, victimize, stigmatize, or pejoratively characterize them on the basis of personal, intellectual, or cultural diversity."

Campus codes corresponding to a second model focus on speech that causes emotional distress. At the University of Texas, students can be punished for engaging in "extreme or outrageous acts or communications intended to harass, intimidate, or humiliate a student on account of race, color, or national origin, and that reasonably cause them to suffer severe emotional distress."

A third model bans speech that causes a hostile or intimidating environment. The University of Michigan code bans speech that "creates an intimidating, hostile, or demeaning environment . . . on the basis of race, ethnicity, religion, sex, sexual orientation, creed, national origin, ancestry, age, marital status, or handicap status."

On many campuses, students are issued guides explaining what is con-

DAVID GOTHARD

SEXIST HARASSMENT

Sexist harassment of women is one of the key themes in the troubling pattern of intolerance on campus. Sexist harassment ranges from sexual innuendo or inappropriate comments — often in the guise of humor — to verbal harassment, inappropriate touching, subtle pressure for sexual activity, and coerced sexual relations.

A typical example of such sexist harassment is a practice called "scoping," in which college men publicly describe and rate women's attractiveness. On several campuses, college men regularly sit at tables next to the cafeteria line. As women go through the line, the men loudly assess their attributes and hold up rating signs ranging from one to ten. In several instances, there are reports that women have chosen to avoid the embarrassment of running this offensive gauntlet either by skipping meals or finding other places to eat.

No reliable survey exists to gauge the extent of sexist harassment on campuses nationwide. But surveys taken on several campuses suggest that the problem is widespread. A 1986 survey at Cornell University, for example, found that 78 percent of the women students had experienced sexist comments and 68 percent had received unwelcome attention from their male peers — most often individuals rather than group harassment. In another survey taken at the University of Rhode Island, 70 percent of the women said they had been insulted by men's sexist remarks.

"Peer harassment sends the message that a woman is not being taken seriously as a person," write Jean O'Gorman Hughes and Bernice Sandler in a report entitled *Peer Harassment: Hassles for Women on Campus,* which is distributed by the Association of American Colleges. "When men harass with impunity, the implication is that women are fair game and that such harassment is acceptable behavior. Just as institutions should prevent and deal with instances of racial harassment, they should also prevent and deal with instances of peer harassment based on sex."

leeway in enacting stricter standards of speech than those that apply in American society as a whole.

"You have to set up something that tells students what the limits are, what they can do, and what they can't do," says Canetta Ivey, a Stanford student who serves on the university's Council of Presidents. "We don't put as many restrictions on freedom of speech as we should. What we are proposing is not completely in line with the First Amendment. I'm not sure it should be. We at Stanford are trying to set a different standard from what society at large is trying to accomplish."

WHAT CRITICS SAY

Critics of the private-sector solution divide into two camps. Some are convinced that leaving the task of restricting offensive speech to institutional gatekeepers such as D.J.'s and media executives is wholly inadequate, a guarantee that more offensive messages will be permitted. To others, the chief reason for concern about private-sector sanctions is that they amount to censorship in a different guise and have the same damaging effects as official restrictions on speech.

Those who regard the private-sector solution as woefully inadequate are convinced that the failure of the entertainment industry to police itself has given rise to the problem. At a time when so many people are eager to make a buck doing whatever is profitable, the temptation to permit messages that cross over the bounds of decency is irresistible — whether the message takes the form of Andrew Dice Clay's comedy routines, 2 Live Crew's misogynist lyrics, or late-night cable TV programs that invite viewers to call 1-900-INCEST for phone fantasies.

Leaving the task of patrolling boundaries to media executives, in this view,

---

sidered offensive speech or verbal harassment. At the University of Michigan, the Office of Affirmative Action issued a guide in 1988 describing which kinds of speech are prohibited and may lead to sanctions. Examples of sanctionable conduct include distributing flyers containing racist threats in residence halls and writing racist graffiti on the door of an Asian woman's study carrel. It is also discriminatory harassment, says the guide, when a male student remarks in a classroom that "Women just aren't as good in this field as men," thus creating a hostile learning environment

for females. You are a harasser, says the guide, when you tell jokes about gay men and women, when your student organization sponsors entertainment that includes a comedian who slurs Hispanics, or when you display a Confederate flag on the door of your room.

While state-supported institutions such as the University of Michigan are required to keep campus policies in line with recent Supreme Court interpretations of the First Amendment, private colleges such as Stanford have greater

> "If reporters shy away from controversy because an ill-chosen word may cause an avalanche of criticism, journalism will become blander, and public discussion about sensitive subjects will be sharply diminished."

is like assigning the foxes to watch the chickens. The purpose of the public sector, say critics of the second choice, is to accomplish what the private sector is unable to do. It is unrealistic, many feel, to assume that parents can effectively patrol the records their children hear and the films they see in a society awash in offensive messages. To stop the tide of toxic messages, they conclude, the force of the laws should be put behind the conviction that certain messages must be restricted.

Besides, note critics of private-sector restrictions, devices such as the motion picture ratings system are ineffective. In many neighborhoods, kids are rarely turned away from a theatre for being underage. Even young children can view most movies on cable or put a cassette into the home VCR. Several years ago, Purdue University researcher Glenn Sparks surveyed 5- to 7-year-old children in suburban Cleveland. Twenty percent said they had seen *Friday the 13th*, and almost half reported they had seen *Poltergeist* — in most cases, on cable television. Rather than shielding impressionable young viewers from offensive material, the ratings system serves mainly to protect the movie industry from public criticism.

Others disapprove of private-sector sanctions for quite a different reason. As they see it, if private firms such as TV networks take it upon themselves to apply sanctions more often, such actions will produce a chilling effect just like the one produced by official censorship — an atmosphere in which speakers and performers muzzle themselves.

Critics note that the Andy Rooney incident appears to have caused just this kind of self-censorship. Several months after he returned to the program, Rooney was preparing commentary for "60 Minutes" on a philanthropist's $50-million gift to the United Negro College Fund. Reportedly, Rooney intended to observe that the existence of separate

black colleges seems a relic of the days of segregation. But Rooney decided not to make the comments, and the piece never aired. "I decided it was so touchy I'd better not do it," Rooney says. "In view of my problems, I decided not to push it."

From this perspective, Rooney's problems are *our* problems. If reporters shy away from controversy because an ill-chosen word may cause an avalanche of criticism and temporary banishment, say critics of private-sector sanctions, journalism will become blander and public discussion about sensitive subjects such as race, gender, and nationality will be sharply diminished.

"I have this vision of America," writes David Boldt of the *Philadelphia Inquirer*, who was the target of a recent uproar over editorial page comments about black women and contraceptives, "with all 250 million of us standing up to our chins in sewage and everyone's saying, 'Don't make waves.'"

There is another reason, critics note,

The film rating system: Does it protect young viewers from offensive material or protect the industry from criticism?

to be wary about condoning private-sector restrictions on speech. The First Amendment forbids only the government from interfering with free expression. Almost no statutes exist to safeguard the speech of individuals in the private sector. Because the protection of the First Amendment does not extend into the private sector, conclude critics of this approach, we need to be especially careful about condoning further restrictions in this area.

SPEECH CODES AREN'T THE ANSWER

Critics of private-sector sanctions are especially concerned about campus speech codes. Most critics don't minimize the problem of bigoted or hateful speech in America's universities. But they feel strongly that such regulations — and the sanctions they define — are dangerously inappropriate ways to deal with it.

"For colleges not to deal with racial prejudice on campus is an abdication of their responsibility in a free society," acknowledges Ira Glasser, executive director of the American Civil Liberties Union (ACLU). "They've got to address those things, but not this way, both because it doesn't work and because it's incompatible with freedom of speech."

As critics of private-sector sanctions point out, when racial hatred or sexist harassment leads to physical assault, colleges should call the police and file a complaint. But trying to prevent hateful speech or verbal harassment by enacting restrictive speech codes is wrongheaded, a violation of the spirit of the First Amendment.

REDEFINING SEXUAL HARASSMENT: FEMINO-PURITANISM IN THE SCHOOLS

The best story in the newspapers of July 20 was not the sentencing of Pete Rose, the opening of the Nixon Presidential Library, or the salvaging of the Civil Rights Bill. It was Michelle Locke's story on the new sexual-harassment code at Amherst-Pelham Regional High School in Massachusetts.

Here's how Locke began: "High schoolers who beam sexually charged stares at their classmates or exchange snippets of intimate gossip in the halls could run afoul of new guidelines designed to curb sexual harassment among students." By the time the last line rolled by ("We're certainly not puritans," a school official said), I was convinced that Locke's piece and the Amherst code itself should go directly into a time capsule. This would give our baffled descendants an outside chance to comprehend some of the strange social obsessions of the 1990s.

I phoned the superintendent of schools, Gus Sayer. Is there a serious harassment problem at the school? No, he said, we just thought these rules were a good idea. How much gazing or leering would it take to be brought up on sexual-harassment charges? There is no time limit, he said. A single stare might do it. And what if a student told a friend, "I think Marcie and Allen have something going"? "That would qualify as sexual harassment," he replied.

This expansive view of harassment is in the air these days. Driven by feminist ideology, we have constantly extended the definition of what constitutes illicit male behavior. Very ambiguous incidents are now routinely flattened out into male predation and firmly listed under date rape. In Swarthmore College's rape-prevention program, "inappropriate innuendo" is actually regarded as an example of acquaintance rape. At the University of Michigan, sexual-harassment

charges were filed against a male student who slipped the following joke under the door of a female student: "Q: How many men does it take to mop a floor? A: None, it's a woman's job."

Now this stern new femino-puritanism seems to be reaching down into the high schools. Looking and talking can apparently be as threatening at Amherst-Pelham as mopping jokes at Michigan. The high school lists all the possible consequences of harassment: Parent conference, apology to victim, detention, suspension, recommendation for expulsion, referral to police.

If I were in charge of a national program to ruin sex for the next generation, I would certainly want to include Amherst-Pelham's new rules. The code is a rich compost of anti-sex messages: males are predatory; sex is so dangerous that chitchat about it can get you brought up on charges; hormone-driven gazing at girls will bring the adult world down on your neck. The most harmful mes-

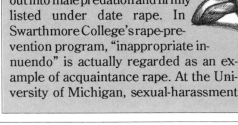

sage, perhaps, is that women are victims; incapable of dismissing creeps with a simple "Buzz off, Bozo," they must be encouraged to run to the administration and say, "Someone was looking at me." And since hallway sex gossip is likely to get to authorities through the services of snitches, friends should probably not be trusted. Far better to talk about the weather.

A small irony here is that gossip is the primary means by which an informal social group, such as a class or a student body, creates and maintains norms. A male who treats females badly is far more likely to be brought into line by peer-group gossip than by a huffy administration imposing rules from above.

Last week's *Economist* featured an interesting lead editorial titled "America's decadent puritans." As it happens, most of the hallmarks of social decline mentioned in the piece are illustrated or strongly implied in the foolish Amherst harassment rules: the itch to censor; litigiousness and endless hearings over the problems of everyday life; the obsession with self-esteem and victimization; the constant truckling to pressure groups; the gradual assertion of a conformist and politically correct way of thinking; the expectation that the courts, the politicians, or somebody will supply us with a stress-free life ("I guess the people in our school are trying to make it a perfect world," an Amherst-Pelham student said to Michelle Locke). That's why these rules are ideal for a time capsule. Let's just stuff them there and skip the whole idea of imposing them on the unsuspecting young.

Excerpted and reprinted with permission from a column by John Leo, U.S. News and World Report, *August 13, 1990, p. 17.*

> "Guardians of political correctness are ready to invoke the heavy artillery of institutional sanctions against anyone suspected of verbal insensitivity."

That is why the ACLU has opposed campus speech codes in Michigan, New York, California, Connecticut, and Wisconsin. In 1989, a federal judge upheld the ACLU's position in the case of the University of Michigan's speech code, on the grounds that it was overly broad and vague. To illustrate its concern, the court cited a case in which a student in a dentistry class said he heard that minority students had a difficult time in the course. The minority professor teaching the course filed a complaint alleging that the comment was unfair and damaged her chances for tenure.

As critics see it, even the University of Michigan's revised speech code, written in response to the Court's concerns, raises serious questions. The interim code, which bars "verbal slurs" based on race, ethnicity, religion, sex, sexual orientation, creed, national origin, ancestry, age, and handicap, and prohibits "unwelcome sexual advances," is too vague to serve any productive purpose. It is more likely to lead to wrangles over what constitutes a violation than it is to stimulate efforts to change the underlying attitudes.

Critics are troubled by the argument that insensitive speech is not simply offensive but harmful, an act of psychological violence. And they are concerned about the implications of judging all messages by their potential to offend. Once private-sector institutions start to value the sensitivity of a statement over its truth, says David Rieff, "all interactions — and for that matter, all institutions — are going to be judged on the basis of their contributions to people's sense of psychological well-being."

ILL-CONCEIVED REMEDY

As critics see it, there are four reasons why campus codes are a bad idea and an ill-conceived remedy to the problem of offensive speech. In each of these respects, say critics, the drawbacks of campus codes illustrate the

Political correctness: New enlightenment on campus or a new form of McCarthyism?

deficiencies of private-sector efforts to restrict offensive speech:

- By driving such speech underground, we miss its message, making it harder to combat the underlying attitudes.
- Since campus rules on permissible speech are vague, they tend to be unevenly enforced, thus inviting the arbitrary exercise of power.
- Speech codes are a constricting intellectual influence on campus, where open-mindedness and freedom of expression should be paramount values.
- Codes focus on symptoms, rather than the underlying problem of prejudice and insensitivity.

Addressing the first of these concerns, Nadine Strossen, professor at the New York University Law School, remarks that "Ugly as it is, this speech undoubtedly has the beneficial result of raising public consciousness about our society's endemic racism. By driving clear expression of racism underground, we make it harder to combat the attitudes it expresses."

However ugly, racist or misogynist epithets are, and however painful they

are for the individuals at whom they are hurled, say critics of speech codes, we learn something from hearing such remarks. If we are protected from bad ideas, ask critics of campus codes, how will we learn to identify them and respond to them?

A second reason for not restricting speech through private-sector measures is that the language of such restrictions gives authorities considerable discretion in determining which words will be censored. "When you pass a rule that represses speech," says Ira Glasser, "you're passing a rule whose sweep is going to be broader than the things you're trying to contain."

Judging by the language of some campus codes, critics maintain, there is little that does not come under their purview. Faced with a lawsuit that challenged its legality, the University of Connecticut was forced to rewrite a code that prohibited "inappropriately directed laughter, inconsiderate jokes, and conspicuous exclusion of students from conversations." Such examples, say critics, show that former governor of Louisiana Huey Long was right when he said that, if fascism comes to America,

University of Michigan students protest against anti-Semitic messages in *The Michigan Daily.*

it will be in the guise of anti-fascism.

Critics point out that granting the censor's power to authorities — public or private — strikes at the heart of free speech values. For this reason, say opponents of speech codes, what is widely regarded as a new enlightenment on campus about insensitive speech is more accurately regarded as a new form of McCarthyism. Self-appointed guardians of what is sensitive and tolerant reserve the right to stand in judgment of everyone else, and are prepared to punish offenders with the cudgels put at their disposal by speech codes.

As critics see it, those who detect the slightest whiff of racism insist on having the last word. That clearly stifles legitimate expression of differences, on campus and elsewhere. The problem, says Andy Rooney, is that "There's almost nothing strong and definite you can say these days without being accused of being racist, sexist, or biased against some element of our society. I must confess that I do think races, nations, sexes, and age groups have some differences, each from the others. If you agree there are differences, do you agree that some characteristics are more desirable than

others? If you do, are you a racist?"

THREAT TO ACADEMIC FREEDOM

Even though campus codes may not violate the First Amendment, say their opponents, they exert a constricting intellectual influence.

"In the Western world," writes Chester Finn, professor of education and public policy at Vanderbilt University, "the university has historically been the locus of the freest expression to be found anywhere. Private colleges, which are not formally bound by the Bill of Rights, are heirs to an even older tradition. For centuries, the campus has been a sanctuary in which knowledge and truth might be pursued — and imparted — with impunity, no matter how popular, distasteful, or politically heterodox the process might sometimes be. That is the essence of academic freedom.

"Having enjoyed almost untrammeled freedom of thought and expression for three and a half centuries," continues Finn, "American colleges and universities are now muzzling themselves. The anti-discrimination and anti-harassment

rules delimit what can be said and done on campus. Inevitably, this must govern what can be taught and written in lab, library, and lecture hall, as well as the sordid antics of fraternity houses and the crude nastiness of inebriated teenagers."

As critics see it, as soon as sensitivity to the feelings of those who are criticized takes precedence over free expression of ideas on American campuses, the fundamental task of the university has been subverted. "The dominant principle of a university," says Benno C. Schmidt, president of Yale University, "must be freedom of thought. We cannot censor or suppress speech, no matter how obnoxious its content, without violating the principle that is our justification for existence."

That, critics note, leads to a final problem with campus speech codes, and with other private-sector restrictions on offensive speech. By focusing on curbing offensive speech, they divert attention from the fundamental problems, racism and sexism. Imposing restrictive codes inspired by a vision of political correctness is not likely, critics observe, to prevent the spread of hatred or intolerance.

In the words of Leonard Steinhorn and Louise Arkel, authors of the People for the American Way report on campus ethnoviolence, "Many schools avoid searching for the cause of the problem and instead turn to quick-fix solutions. Too many schools abdicate their most basic role — to educate, to teach students to think critically and challenge easy answers and assumptions. Restricting free speech may contribute to an atmosphere of intolerance, and to an impression that some rights can be short-circuited to protect others."

To advocates of a third perspective on free speech, to which we now turn, a more promising alternative is recognizing our obligation to find ways to encourage *more* speech rather than imposing rules designed to restrict speech. ∎

CHOICE #3
FIRST PRINCIPLES AND FREE EXPRESSION: MORE SPEECH, NOT ENFORCED SILENCE

"Because speaking freely is the cornerstone of our liberties, freedom of expression should be abridged rarely, if at all. The best remedy for offensive messages is not restrictions but more speech."

At a time of moral disorientation, many Americans are troubled by a sense that anything goes, that nothing is sacred, and that a tide of offensive messages poses an increasing threat. In response, there is growing support across the political spectrum for restricting offensive speech, which looks to many people like the only way to stem the tide.

But advocates of a third perspective disagree. Far from calling for additional restraints on speech — either legal or institutional — they call for more open expression. "Today," says attorney Donna Demac, author of a recent book entitled *Liberty Denied: The Current Rise of Censorship in America*, "the United States faces the significant challenge of restoring the traditions of free speech that have been eroded in the 1980s."

The Bill of Rights is often referred to as the fundamental charter of American liberties, and for good reason, say proponents of this third choice. The ten amendments contained in it were de-signed to restrict the role and authority of the government. It is no coincidence, say advocates of this choice, that the very first amendment specifies that "Congress shall make no law . . . abridging the freedom of speech." As Justice Benjamin Cardozo asserted, "Freedom of speech is the indispensable condition of nearly every other form of freedom."

That is the point of departure for our third perspective, which advocates a strict interpretation of the First Amendment, a view described by Justice Hugo Black when he said "I take 'no law abridging' to mean no law abridging." One of our distinguishing features as a society, insist people who take this position, is a staunch defense of individual freedom, which begins with the freedom to think and say what we please, without fear of censorship — whether the restrictions on speech are official or result from private-sector action. Not only may Congress "make no law abridging the freedom of speech," say advocates of this third view, it must also preserve that freedom against those who would abridge it.

DAVID GOTHARD

Those who favor a strict interpretation of the First Amendment believe that freedom of expression should be abridged only in rare instances, if at all. Advocates of this view generally oppose anything that would restrict or prohibit free expression and they offer a simple reply to those who would do so. "The remedy to be applied," as Justice Brandeis observed, "is more speech, not enforced silence."

Since they view speaking freely as the cornerstone of our freedoms, advocates of this third perspective insist that we restrict freedom of expression at our peril. The greater harm lies not in the effects of objectionable speech, they believe, but in restricting speech.

TYRANNY OF THE MAJORITY

It is dangerously beside the point, say defenders of a strict interpretation of the First Amendment, to justify censorship on the grounds that a majority supports cracking down on objectionable speech. In the words of Aryeh Neier, former head of the American Civil Liberties Union, "That a majority of people in a community say they don't want to see or hear something is no legal basis for suppressing it. You could suppress virtually anything if all you had to do was submit it to a vote. Our Constitution says that 'Congress shall make no law abridging the freedom of speech.' That is, the democratic process shall not prohibit *any* speech or expression."

Above all, say civil libertarians, the First Amendment is a tool for protecting minority views against the tyranny of the majority. Minority views, even when they are offensive — or more accurately, *especially* when they are offensive — deserve to be protected. Our commitment to protect minority views is one of our most distinctive and praiseworthy values as a society.

That, say advocates of this view, is why neither 2 Live Crew nor Andrew

Dice Clay nor other entertainers with offensive messages should be censored. Defending them doesn't mean you like their message. In the words of writer Martha Frankel, "Those of us concerned about First Amendment issues must defend 2 Live Crew's right to make music. But we don't have to pretend that what they have to offer is more than vile drivel with a backbeat."

With the exception of child pornography, where minors are exploited against their will, there is no justification for permitting government to decide what images we can see or what lyrics will be heard. Above all, from this point of view, no individual or government official should be permitted to be the arbiter of taste or public morality.

As columnist Charles Krauthammer

writes, "Although you may prefer not to express yourself by dancing naked on a runway in a bar, some people do, and you have no business stopping them. Nor do you have any business trying to stop those who like to sit by the runway and imbibe in this form of expression. It may not be *Swan Lake*, but the First Amendment does not hinge on judgments of artistic merit."

There is no question, say critics of government censorship, that free speech imposes a cost. The Bill of Rights is not for the fainthearted nor for those who think government should serve as a hall monitor, shielding us from messages we would prefer not to hear. "The price we pay for freedom of expression," says Danny Goldberg, a manager of rock acts and chairman of the ACLU Foundation in Southern California, "is that some things will be considered vile by some people." But a certain discomfort with offensive messages is a small price to pay for the freedom to say what we please. To advocates of this perspective, a strict defense of free speech makes sense for several reasons, one of which is the encouragement of creativity. Consider the range of artistic expression in this nation and the achievements of Americans in creative writing, painting, music, dance, theater, and cinema. In countries where the government curbs freedom of speech, artists are considered instruments of state

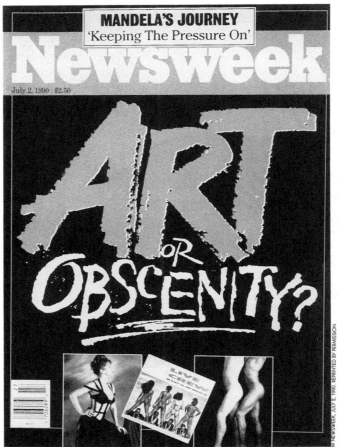

"The First Amendment teaches an important lesson: we must restrain the impulse to silence what is threatening or strange, and thus acknowledge our diversity as a community."

DAVID GOTHARD

policy. If their messages are not consistent with the party line, they are often regarded as dangerous and dissident voices that must be harnessed or silenced.

Though it is rarely acknowledged, say advocates of this position, the creativity of Americans in many areas is a result of a cultural environment in which a wide range of expression is allowed to flourish. To advocates of a strict interpretation of the First Amendment, restricting artistic freedom is a grave mistake. In the words of Joe Saltzman, faculty member at the School of Journalism at the University of California, Los Angeles, "Artists — whether they be writers, photographers, painters, comedians, or musicians — should be able to shock their audiences into new areas of feeling or thinking. Original styles often look crude and excessive. It has been proven again and again that it is the offensive artist who leads us into brave new worlds. The point is that these people have something to say. That is why — no matter how many Americans despise their art — their work should be protected by the First Amendment and encouraged by any responsible citizen."

A second benefit of free speech is the exploration of unsettling ideas. Defenders of free speech acknowledge that those who test the public's tolerance are often a disreputable lot, including pornographers, Nazis, and spokesmen for the Aryan Resistance. "Rarely are centrist groups denied their First Amendment rights," says Aryeh Neier. "The right to free speech is always tested at the extremes."

Why should we care about the right to express racist messages or sexually explicit material, which serve no apparent socially useful purpose? ACLU lawyer Barry Lynn maintains that, if sexually explicit material did not promote controversial ideas, it would not provoke such an angry response.

The same thing could be said about the Metzgers' cable TV program, "Race and Reason," or about violent images in film and television. As movie critic Pauline Kael wrote two decades ago in praise of *Bonnie and Clyde*, which attracted attention because of its graphic violence: "The dirty reality of death, not suggestions but blood and holes, is necessary. It is a kind of violence that

says something to us. It is something that movies must be free to use."

Advocates of this perspective are concerned about any action that denounces writers for their point of view and shuts off debate, such as the decision of CBS executives to suspend Andy Rooney for his comments about gays and blacks. Responding to the "60 Minutes" incident, Howard Kurtz, who covers media for the *Washington Post*, commented that Andy Rooney's comments "may be insensitive, muddled, or just plain wrongheaded. But does that warrant journalistic excommunication? Do the thought police have to make an arrest for every real or imagined transgression? There is plenty of room for vigorous disagreement on these volatile issues for columns and commentaries and op-ed attacks and talk-show tantrums that tackle the subject with no holds barred. But denouncing writers and shutting off the debate will not make the problems go away. If journalism becomes increasingly allergic to controversy, increasingly wary of telling people uncomfortable truths, that will simply create a vacuum to be filled with rumor, whispers, and prejudice."

The same logic, say advocates of free speech, extends to campus speech codes. Proponents of this third choice believe that efforts to outlaw ugly or insensitive remarks will inevitably endanger the right to express other uncomfortable ideas.

We are obliged to honor the spirit of the First Amendment and the civics lesson it is intended to teach, say advocates of this choice. The commitment to free speech reminds communities that they must deal with uncomfortable social and political situations; the White Aryan Resistance will not go away just because its cable TV program is not allowed. By restraining the impulse to silence what is threatening or strange, we acknowledge our diversity as a community.

As advocates of free speech point out, the First Amendment was meant to benefit not only speakers but listeners. The right to listen to wide-ranging debate is every bit as important as the right to speak one's mind. The public, in this view, has a need to know and a need to test accepted, but possibly outworn, ideas against new ones. That requires the airing of competing viewpoints. If we are serious about improving the quality of public education and civic discourse, say advocates of this choice, we are obliged to protect the right to debate conflicting views.

Advocates of this perspective acknowledge that free speech imposes a heavy obligation. As Gerald Gunther, a constitutional law professor at Stanford University, remarked in a debate about speech codes on that campus, "The refusal to suppress offensive speech is one of the most difficult obligations the free speech principle imposes. Yet it is also one of the First Amendment's greatest glories, and it is a central test of a community's commitment to free speech."

STICKS AND STONES

From this perspective, few forms of speech — neither pornography nor violence in film and television, nor offensive rap or rock lyrics, nor the ravings of the White Aryan Resistance — pose a real danger to us as individuals or as a society.

That was the point of a February 1991 Georgia Supreme Court ruling. At issue was a state law that went into effect in 1987 prohibiting bumper stickers and emblems bearing lewd or offensive messages, particularly those describing sexual acts, excretory functions, or parts of the human body. James Daniel Cunningham of Smyrna, Georgia, was arrested for violating the law when he

displayed a decal on the rear door of his van bearing a vulgar variation of the phrase "stuff happens." Writing for the court, Chief Justice Harold G. Clarke struck down the law on the grounds that "The peace of society is not endangered by the profane or lewd word which is not directed at a particular audience."

As the nursery rhyme reminds us, "Sticks and stones may break your bones, but words will never hurt you." Offending people with insensitive words, insist defenders of a strict interpretation of the First Amendment, is not the same as causing physical injury. The assertion that words cause psychic injury leads to the wholly unjustified conclusion, in Lewis Lapham's phrase, that we should "place speech and symbolic gesture in the same category of objects as the tire iron, the nightstick, and the truncheon."

The urge to restrict certain messages, say advocates of a strict interpretation of the First Amendment, also reflects a lack of faith in the ability of individuals to judge for themselves. The First Amendment rests on what constitutional scholar Archibald Cox refers to as "faith in the ultimate good sense and decency of free people." If you think adults are unable to resist the messages of pornographers, advertisers, and political extremists, say advocates of this choice, it may make sense to shield everyone from certain kinds of messages. But this, says *Chicago Tribune* editorial writer Stephen Chapman, is "an approach worthy of a nation of children." To advocates of this third perspective, it is not what the framers of the Bill of Rights had in mind.

As the American Library Association put it in the organization's statement on the freedom to read, "We are deeply concerned about these attempts at suppression. Most such attempts rest on a denial of the fundamental premise of democracy: that the ordinary citizen, by exercising critical judgment, will accept the good and reject the bad. The censors, public and private, assume that

> "Ordinary citizens by exercising critical judgment, will accept the good and reject the bad."
> — American Library Association

they should determine what is good and what is bad for their fellow citizens. We trust Americans to recognize propaganda, and to reject it. We do not believe they need the help of censors to assist them in this task."

Every time speech is restricted, say advocates of this choice, our freedom to control our own lives is jeopardized. As attorney and feminist Wendy Kaminer puts it, explaining why feminists should not support censorship of pornography, "We cannot look to the government to rid us of pornography. The feminist movement against pornography must remain an anti-defamation movement involved in education and consciousness-raising. Legislative or judicial control of pornography is simply not possible without breaking down the legal principles and procedures that are essential to our own right to speak and, ultimately, our freedom to control our own lives."

CENSORSHIP IS CONTAGIOUS

When advocates of restricting offensive speech ask what would be lost by silencing extreme voices, such as avowed Nazis or violent films or TV programs, advocates of strict First Amendment rights have a ready answer. Every act of censorship, they believe, begets other such acts. "Censorship," says free-speech lawyer Floyd Abrams, "is contagious. Censorship is habit-forming."

Certain forms of speech cannot be restricted without threatening the principle of free speech and the right of minorities to speak their views, argue advocates of the third choice. For this reason, concludes the ACLU's Ira Glasser, it is Jews who should be most fervent about defending the rights of Nazis, and blacks who should care most about defending the rights of the Klan.

People who fear the "slippery slope" of censorship recall the McCarthy era as a cautionary lesson, a reminder that

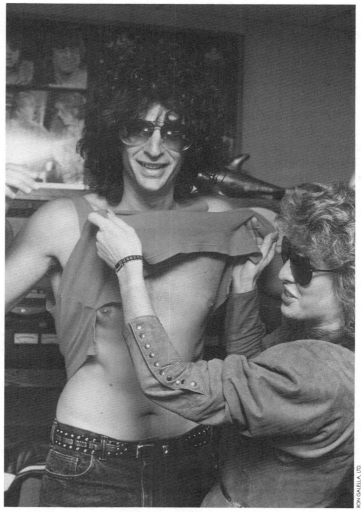

"Shock Jock" Howard Stern: The FCC has warned him and other disc jockeys to clean up their acts.

freedom of expression is by no means to be taken for granted. In the heyday of Senator Joseph McCarthy, scholars, writers, filmmakers, civil servants, and others were publicly castigated, and their lives and careers were destroyed by allegations of Communist sympathies.

Today, many civil libertarians fear that a censorship mentality once again poses a threat to our freedom. They point, for example, to recent FCC restrictions on material deemed unsuitable for radio broadcast. Going beyond its earlier prohibition on the use of "seven dirty words," the FCC now has a policy of punishing any radio station that allows "patently offensive language" — a more comprehensive, imprecise, and judgmental standard.

Advocates of free speech fear that, as a result of the FCC's crackdown on "shock radio," freedom of expression over the airwaves will be curtailed. As Monroe Price, law school dean at Yeshiva University observes, "the threat to broadcasting licenses worth tens and hundreds of millions of dollars — and the prospect of federal prosecution — will have its intended chilling effect."

What concerns civil libertarians is that the chill could eventually extend to programming on divisive political issues, curtailing the range of viewpoints expressed.

Civil libertarians also cite such examples as the passage in 1985 of a stringent obscenity law in North Carolina. In the new mood of strict enforcement ushered in by passage of the law, a 21-year-old clerk in a convenience store was arrested after selling two magazines to an undercover policeman. A jury determined that the magazines were obscene and convicted the sales clerk. Subsequently, the judge sentenced her to six years in jail and a $10,000 fine.

RISING TIDE OF RESTRAINT

Once the idea of protecting the public from potentially harmful ideas catches on, say advocates of unfettered expression, there is no telling how far it will go. But recent examples provide a glimpse of what we have to fear. In 1987, for example, a school superintendent in Bay County, Florida, who was concerned about the supposedly unhealthy influence of certain educational materials, banned 64 books and plays from the district's schools. Among the works were Shakespeare's *Twelfth Night* and *The Merchant of Venice*, Hemingway's *The Old Man and the Sea*, F. Scott Fitzgerald's *The Great Gatsby*, and other classics. It wasn't until a group of parents, teachers, and students took the case to court that most, but not all, of the titles were once again permitted in Bay County classrooms.

Advocates of this choice acknowledge that censorship of this sort is nothing new. But, according to several groups that track efforts to censor school materials, censorship attempts have been on the rise since the early 1980s. As Judith Krug, director of the American Library Association's Office of Intellectual Freedom, points out, those who favor censorship of certain kinds of material are a more varied group than would-be censors were a few years ago. Today's censors include not only cultural conservatives but women's groups and ethnic minorities pushing to restrict or rewrite materials which, in their view, contain racist or sexist references.

The materials banned in at least some districts include Mark Twain's *Huckleberry Finn* and J. D. Salinger's *Catcher in the Rye*, John Steinbeck's *Grapes of Wrath*, Judy Blume's books for young adults, the swimsuit issue of *Sports Illustrated*, and a Caldecott-award-winning version of *Little Red Riding Hood*, which was banned in some communities on the grounds that grandmother had a glass of wine after escaping the wolf. The bannings also include psychology and

Banned books: "Protecting the public" against *Little Red Riding Hood* and classics of American literature

biology textbooks, and a sexual abuse prevention book entitled *You Can Say No*. Protectors of free speech are especially concerned about the fact that some publishers, in an effort to avoid courtroom battles over censorship, have omitted potentially offensive material from texts, such as the mention of evolution in biology textbooks.

JUST SAY NO

When confronted with offensive messages, what course of action is consistent with the commitment to free speech? One of the most effective responses, say advocates of this third choice, is simply to turn away.

Many civil libertarians support laws to prevent what is known as "thrusting" — the display of offensive speech in a way that violates the privacy of passersby. Such laws include ordinances regulating the way adult bookstores advertise their wares.

Beyond that, say civil libertarians, most offensive messages can be ignored. If you find certain TV programs offensive, change the channel or turn off the television. If you are offended by certain magazines in a local newsstand, don't buy them. In the words of rapper Ice-T: "This should be the bottom line. If you don't like 2 Live Crew, you don't have to listen to them, you don't have to buy their album, and you don't have to go see them in concert. But the government and the courts should not be de-

> "If ideas are too important to suppress, they are also too important to ignore. The whole point of free speech is not to make ideas exempt from criticism but to expose them to it."
>
> — Garry Wills

ciding what we can and cannot listen to, what we can and cannot buy, or what 2 Live Crew can rap about." In the interest of protecting children, argue advocates of the third choice, parents have an obligation to listen to lyrics on records their children bring home; and they have a duty to talk to them about what is wrong with certain messages. They also have the right to refuse to buy offensive materials for their children, the right to call local radio stations and complain when offensive messages are broadcast, and the right to switch stations.

SPEAKING UP, SPEAKING OUT

Advocates of unfettered speech point out that protecting a person's right to express their views is quite a different thing from saying "I don't care what views you express." The First Amendment imposes an obligation not just to tolerate the expression of views you disagree with, but to counter those views, to voice your disapproval, and to call on others to voice their disapproval. "If ideas are too important to suppress," says Garry Wills, "they are also too important to ignore. The whole point of free speech is not to make ideas exempt from criticism but to expose them to it."

Far from being a weak or toothless remedy, say advocates of this option, voicing one's disapproval of offensive messages is strong medicine. Andrew Dice Clay's popularity as a performer started to decline, they argue, when "Saturday Night Live" cast member Nora Dunn and singer Sinead O'Connor refused to perform on the same show with him, on the grounds that his routine — in Dunn's words — is "degrading and repulsive." Many people in publishing started to have second thoughts about Bret Ellis's lurid book *American Psycho* when female members of the Simon and Schuster's editorial staff, as well as members of the sales staff, spoke out against its gratuitous vio-

lence, and artist George Corsillo, who was supposed to do artwork for the cover, refused.

Such responses, say advocates of this choice, are entirely consistent with the spirit of the First Amendment. The way to deal with offensive messages is not to censor them, nor to impose institutional restrictions, but to respond by countering offensive messages with other points of view.

This strategy applies not just to offensive books, rap lyrics, and comedy routines, but also to offensive speech on campus.

Robb Flynn of heavy metal band Vio-lence: If you don't like the message, say civil libertarians, you can turn away from it or speak out against it.

THE ROOT OF THE PROBLEM

From this perspective, campus leaders confronted by incidents of hateful or hurtful speech have an obligation not only to protect the right to express offensive views, but also to deal with the problem by taking efforts to curtail racism and sexism. It is essential, say advocates of this choice, to recognize and deal with the root of the problem, not just the offensive speech which is a symptom.

At the University of Massachusetts at Amherst, where a racial brawl in 1986 injured 10 students, university officials recognize that, while speech codes may suppress bigoted remarks, they do nothing to change bigoted thoughts. "We have to realize," says Grant Ingle, the university's director of human relations, "that students come to the university having had driver's education and physical education but not multicultural education. Many students from segregated communities come to college and encounter a level of diversity for which they are not properly prepared."

The best way for universities to deal with racist attitudes, from this perspective, is not to muzzle their expression but to encourage open discussion about racial differences by sponsoring cultural sensitivity workshops. On a growing number of campuses, including the University of Massachusetts and the University of Wisconsin, measures of this kind are being taken to encourage acceptance of differences.

Civil libertarians acknowledge a potential trap that such courses may consist not of open inquiry but ideological indoctrination, or even attitude adjustment. But, say advocates of unfettered speech, promoting understanding of differences is consistent with the spirit of the First Amendment and the obligation it imposes to deal with offensive speech not with censorship or restrictions but with open discussion.

WHAT CRITICS SAY

Critics disagree sharply with the civil libertarian view of unfettered free speech. The notion that the First Amendment was intended to protect virtually all speech, in the view of critics, is a serious misinterpretation of what the framers of the Bill of Rights had in mind and a misreading of the message of various Supreme Court rulings. Critics point out that the Supreme Court has consistently held that obscenity is *not* protected expression, any more than libel and slander are protected.

Civil libertarians defend unfettered free speech on the grounds that the First Amendment protects the open market-place of ideas and defends artistic freedom. But critics respond that protecting offensive speech by sweeping it under the mantel of artistic freedom stretches the meaning of art beyond recognition.

In the words of columnist George Will, who begins by apologizing for quoting coarse language: "Corporations sell civil pollution for profit. Liberals rationalize it as virtuous tolerance in 'the marketplace of ideas.' Not to worry, yawn the *New York Times* editorialists: 'The history of music is the story of innovative, even outrageous styles that interacted, adapted, and became mainstream.' Oh, I see: First Stravinsky's 'Rite of Spring,' and now 2 Live Crew's 'Me So Horny' ('I won't tell your momma if you don't tell your dad/I know he'll be disgusted when he sees your p—y busted.') Innovative. When that is 'mainstream,' this will be an interesting country."

An appropriate response to such "artistic" expression, say critics, is not tolerance but outrage. To do nothing about such messages because their destructive effect cannot be proven conclusively is both foolhardy and irresponsible.

It is one thing, say critics of this third choice, to tolerate obnoxious messages,

Ku Klux Klan demonstration in Houston: Advocating free speech for groups like the KKK may encourage their hateful message.

which we are all obliged to do. It is quite another to acknowledge the threat posed by blatantly racist, sexist, and hatemongering messages. "At the core of the argument that we should resist all regulation of speech," says Stanford law professor Charles Lawrence, commenting on the need for campus speech codes, "is the ideal that the best cure for bad speech is good, that ideas which affirm equality and the worth of all individuals will ultimately prevail. This is an empty ideal, one that invites calls for restrictions on speech, unless those of us who would fight racism are vigilant and unequivocal in that fight."

Civil libertarians, says Lawrence, typically put a great deal more energy into defending the rights of individuals to say what they please than they put into fighting racism, sexism, or homophobia.

What attorney Marshall Pearlin said a few years ago about the ACLU's decision to protect the rights of Ku Klux Klan members to demonstrate in public applies as well to ACLU efforts to defend the right of the KKK to keep their white supremacist programming on a Kansas City cable TV station. "When you talk abstractly about the First Amendment," says Pearlin, "you ignore the rights of blacks, which are in imminent and real danger now." It is essential, says Pearlin, to acknowledge the threat posed to minority groups by racists. "The Klan is real and the Klan is dangerous," says Pearlin. "We'd better wake up to that before it's too late."

As critics of this third position see it, the assertion that virtually all forms of expression must be permitted at the risk of jeopardizing individual rights represents individualism carried to an unhealthy extreme. What we must do, they insist, is balance individual rights against responsibilities to the community.

Importantly, in this view, the Court has recognized that the needs of the community must take precedence in certain circumstances. Even when films are intended for consenting adults only, the Court said in a June 1973 ruling, "Rights and interests other than those [of individuals who choose to view such materials] are involved. These include the interest of the public in the quality of life, the total community environment, the tone of commerce, and, possibly, the public safety itself."

Unfettered free speech is an admirable principle, say critics. But, in their view, advocates of free speech do not acknowledge the swelling tide of offensive messages and its coarsening, morally desensitizing effects on community life. And that, they conclude, is why certain restrictions must be imposed. ■

GRAPPLING WITH LIMITS: THE LAST WORD ON THE FIRST AMENDMENT

"People disagree about the harm caused by offensive messages and how communities should respond. The question is what we are prepared to tolerate as the price of maintaining our freedoms."

Two hundred years after the Bill of Rights was added to the Constitution, a contentious debate is taking place about the meaning of free speech and the boundaries of acceptable expression. In the words of Lewis Lapham, editor of *Harper's* magazine, "The argument about free speech is as noisy and confused as the bidding in the pit of a commodities exchange. Nobody knows who can say what to whom, or when, or under what circumstances, but almost everyone has some kind of point to make."

The discussion about where to draw the line on free speech and how communities should respond when faced with offensive messages is far from abstract. In many communities, and on hundreds of college campuses, people are struggling to define the boundaries of permissible speech, trying to reach some agreement about how to respond when that boundary is crossed.

The issue, in many cases, is not whether certain messages or images are offensive. In the case of 2 Live Crew lyrics, Andrew Dice Clay's comedy routines, demeaning speech on campus, and the ravings of white supremacist groups, many people agree that they *are* offensive. But what is an appropriate response that is consistent with our commitment to free speech?

In the case of 2 Live Crew, for example, many people agree with Juan Williams that *As Nasty as They Wanna Be* is offensive and that it distorts conceptions of "good sex, good relationships, and good times." But these three perspectives lead to quite different assessments of how communities should respond.

Advocates of legal restrictions on offensive speech favor strict enforcement of existing obscenity laws, and new legal measures to stem the tide of toxic messages. They wholeheartedly approve of the decision of Florida District Court Judge Jose Gonzalez's decision to declare *As Nasty as They Wanna Be* obscene. Extreme instances of free speech must be curbed, they feel, to make community life more whole and wholesome.

Advocates of private-sector restrictions take a different view of how to deal with corrosive messages such as 2 Live Crew lyrics. Their response is that musical groups, the people who operate the clubs at which they perform, and the executives of recording firms that distribute their material should exercise more discretion about releasing material that is patently offensive.

Advocates of a strict interpretation of the First Amendment differ both about the extent of the harm caused by offensive messages and how individuals and communities should respond. Even if 2 Live Crew's lyrics amount to "vile drivel with a backbeat," in Martha Frankel's words, the group still has a right to produce such music. People who find the

39

group's message offensive have the right to voice their objections to it. But the group should not be censored, in this view, because limitations on *anyone's* right to free speech threaten *everyone's* right. Advocates of a strict interpretation of the First Amendment conclude that the Bill of Rights protects 2 Live Crew, just as it protects other Americans.

As we have seen, the same array of responses is being debated with regard to a wide range of offensive speech — including racist epithets, raunch radio, and Robert Mapplethorpe's photographs of men in sadomasochistic poses.

CLASHING VALUES

What are the underlying issues in the debate over freedom of expression? In one respect, the question is how we should regard numerous recent instances of offensive words and images. Are they evidence of a society that has lost its moral compass, a society in which everything is permitted and nothing is forbidden? Or are they indications of a healthy respect for free expression and our willingness to pay the price free expression exacts, which is to tolerate messages that are offensive and uncomfortable?

In another respect, this is a debate about how to resolve the tension between contending values. While free speech is important, it is just one of the things we value. Writing about efforts to restrict pornography, Charles Krauthammer comments that the debate about what should be done amounts to a clash over two fundamental values, individual liberty and public morality. Those who favor censorship, says Krauthammer, "are prepared to admit that restrictions curtail liberty, though a kind of liberty they do not think is particularly worth having. On the other hand, civil libertarians admit that a price

of liberty is that it stands to be misused, and that pornography may be one of those misuses. Public morality may suffer, but freedom is more precious. Both sides agree, however, that one cannot have everything and may sometimes have to trade one political good for another."

The debate over free speech is also about the damage caused by offensive words and images. Should they be considered acts of psychological violence — in James Underwood's words, "sordid influences that are every bit as harmful as a blow to the head"? Clearly, speech sometimes hurts and those who are offended or injured by it are often inclined to remove the pain by removing the speech. But if measures are taken to restrict speech that causes discomfort, a great many restrictions would have to be put in place and the right to speak freely might be seriously eroded.

There are also differences about the damage done to individual rights whenever certain kinds of speech are restricted. Those who favor additional restrictions — whether campus speech codes, self-censorship in the recording industry, or laws such as the Memphis ban on public performances involving nudity, sexual conduct, and excess

violence — feel that such measures can be taken without endangering constitutional rights.

For their part, civil libertarians warn that once certain forms of expression are restricted or banned, would-be censors are likely to find other messages that deserve to be censored. If we begin by banning racial epithets on the grounds that they amount to verbal harassment and then move on (as the Colorado legislature has done) to pass a bill prohibiting disparaging comments about perishable fruit, other such measures are likely to follow — and talking freely will soon be a thing of the past. Perhaps, as Floyd Abrams said, censorship *is* contagious. So one of the central questions is whether offensive speech can be restricted without infringing on rights protected by the First Amendment.

If the passionate debate over free speech is a sign of the energizing value of the First Amendment, the divisiveness of the discussion should also be a warning. In an open marketplace of ideas and arguments, disputes are inevitable and even desirable. Yet at times, the debate over free speech threatens to become a shouting match.

At the center of today's debate about free speech is a question that has been posed repeatedly, a question that the framers of the Constitution and the Bill of Rights grappled with 200 years ago: What is a proper and acceptable balance between individual rights and the community's need to maintain order and protect itself from threats to its health and safety? How these conflicting objectives are balanced depends on what we value most, and what we are prepared to tolerate as the price of maintaining our freedoms. ■

"So what if the First Amendment does go? We still have twenty-five more."

FOR FURTHER READING

For historical perspective on the First Amendment, see the American Civil Liberties Union's briefing paper, *Freedom of Expression,* which traces its roots to the Enlightenment era and describes its role in America's constitutional system (New York: The American Civil Liberties Union, 1991).

For reports that reflect growing concern about tasteless, offensive, or socially corrosive messages, see two recent cover stories in *Time* and *Newsweek:* an article by Richard Corliss entitled "X-Rated" that appeared in the May 7, 1990 issue of *Time* magazine, and an article entitled "Violence in Our Culture," which appeared in *Newsweek,* April 1, 1991.

Attorney Donna Demac takes a comprehensive look at what she regards as the growing threat posed by censors in *Liberty Denied: The Current Rise of Censorship in America* (New York: Pen Center, 1988). *Censorship News,* a newsletter published by the New York-based National Coalition Against Censorship, tracks efforts to restrict freedom of expression.

The National Coalition Against Pornography has produced two reports on the evidence of harm; see "Pornography's Relationship to Rape and Aggression Toward Women," and "Consequences of Pornography Consumption" (Cincinnati: National Coalition Against Pornography, 1990). Sociologist Thelma McCormack reviews the evidence on pornography and comes to quite a different conclusion in "Making Sense of Research on Pornography," a report distributed by the National Coalition Against Censorship.

For thoughtful analyses of pornography and the issues it poses, see Linda Williams's *Hard Core: Power, Pleasure, and the "Frenzy of the Visible"* (Berkeley and Los Angeles: University of Califor-

nia Press, 1989); and Donald Alexander Downs's *The New Politics of Pornography* (Chicago: University of Chicago Press, 1989), which examines the Minneapolis and Indianapolis ordinances, and explores the challenge they pose to free speech.

For accounts of hate speech on campus, see *Hate in the Ivory Tower* (Washington, D.C.: People for the American Way, March, 1990), which provides a survey of the wave of intolerance on college campuses and the response to it, and *Campus Ethnoviolence and the Policy Options* (Baltimore: National Institute Against Prejudice and Violence, 1990), a report written by Howard Ehrlich.

For different perspectives on the campus response to hate speech, see Mary Ellen Gale's essay on "Curbing Racial Speech," in the Winter 1990/1991 issue of *The Responsive Community,* an article by Steve French entitled "Hate Goes to College," which appeared in the July 1990 issue of the *ABA Journal,* and "Taking Offense," an article on "political correctness" on campus and the threat it poses to free speech, which appeared in *Newsweek,* December 24, 1990.

In "The Campus: 'An Island of Repression in a Sea of Freedom,'" which appeared in the September, 1989 issue of *Commentary,* Chester E. Finn, Jr. expresses concern about campus codes, arguing that such actions threaten the fundamental principle of open debate.

Mari Matsuda, law professor at Stanford University, is the author of an influential article, "Public Response to Racist Speech: Considering the Victim's Story," which appeared in the *Michigan Law Review* (August, 1989). Matsuda calls for universities to forbid hate speech directed at minorities, on the grounds that freedom of speech was intended to protect the powerless.

For two contrasting perspectives on racist speech, see Charles Lawrence's "If He Hollers Let Him Go: Regulating Racist Speech On Campus," which argues in favor of speech codes; and Nadine Strossen's response, "Regulating Racist Speech On Campus: A Modest Proposal?" which warns against the censoring effects of such codes. Both articles appear in the *Duke Law Journal,* Volume 1990, number 3.

ACKNOWLEDGMENTS

We would like to express our appreciation to the people who helped choose this year's topics and took part in discussions about how they should be approached. Once again, David Mathews and Daniel Yankelovich provided both support and guidance. Our colleagues John Doble, Jean Johnson, Jon Rye Kinghorn, Robert Kingston, Suzanne Morse, Patrick Scully, Jeffrey Tuchman, and Deborah Wadsworth played a valuable role in refining the framework and clarifying the presentation.

Finally, our thanks to Loren Siegel at the American Civil Liberties Union and to Howard J. Ehrlich and Robert D. Purvis of the National Institute Against Prejudice and Violence, who provided advice and assistance as we prepared the manuscript.

NATIONAL ISSUES FORUMS

The National Issues Forums (NIF) program consists of locally initiated Forums and study circles which bring citizens together in communities throughout the nation for nonpartisan discussions about public issues. In these Forums, the traditional town meeting concept is re-created. Each fall and winter, three issues of particular concern are addressed in these groups. The results are then shared with policymakers.

More than 3,000 civic and education organizations — high schools and colleges, libraries, service organizations, religious groups, and other types of groups — convene Forums and study circles in their communities as part of the National Issues Forums. Each participating organization assumes ownership of the program, adapting the NIF approach and materials to its own mission and to the needs of the local community. In this sense, there is no one type of NIF program. There are many varieties, all locally directed and financed.

Here are answers to some of the most frequently asked questions about the National Issues Forums:

WHAT HAPPENS IN FORUMS?

The goal of Forums and study circles is to stimulate and sustain a certain kind of conversation — a genuinely useful conversation that moves beyond the bounds of partisan politics and the airing of grievances to mutually acceptable responses to common problems. Distinctively, Forums invite discussion about each of several choices, along with their cost and the main arguments for and against them. Forum moderators encourage participants to examine their values and preferences — as individuals and as community members — and apply them to specific issues.

CAN I PARTICIPATE IF I'M NOT WELL INFORMED ABOUT THE ISSUE?

To discuss public issues, citizens need to grasp the underlying problem or dilemma, and they should understand certain basic facts and trends. But it isn't necessary to know a great deal about an issue. NIF discussions focus on what public actions should be taken. That's a matter of judgment that requires collective deliberation. The most important thing to ponder and discuss is the kernel of convictions on which each alternative is based. The task of the National Issues Forums is not to help participants acquire a detailed knowledge of the issue but to help people sort out conflicting principles and preferences, to find out where they agree and disagree and work toward common understandings.

ISN'T ONE PERSON'S OPINION AS GOOD AS ANOTHER'S?

Public judgment differs from personal opinion. It arises when people sort out their values and work through hard choices. Public judgment reflects people's views once they have an opportunity to confront an issue seriously, consider the arguments for and against various positions, and come to terms with the consequences of their beliefs.

ARE FORUM PARTICIPANTS EXPECTED TO AGREE UPON A COURSE OF ACTION?

A fundamental challenge in a democratic nation is sustaining a consensus about a broad direction of public action without ignoring or denying the diversity of individual preferences. Forums do not attempt to achieve complete agreement. Rather, their goal is to help

people see which interests are shareable and which are not. A Forum moderator once described the common ground in these words: "Here are five statements that were made in our community Forum. Not everyone agreed with all of them. But there is nothing in them that we couldn't agree with."

WHAT'S THE POINT OF ONE MORE BULL SESSION?

Making choices is hard work. It requires something more than talking about public issues. "Talking about" is what we do every day. We talk about the weather, or our friends, or the government. But the "choice work" that takes place in Forum discussions involves weighing alternatives and considering the consequences of various courses of action. It means accepting certain choices even if they aren't entirely consistent with what we want, and even if the cost is higher than we imagined. Forum participants learn how to work through issues together. That means using talk to discover, not just to persuade or advocate.

DO THE FORUMS LEAD TO POLITICAL ACTION?

Neither local convenors nor the National Issues Forums as a whole advocate partisan positions or specific solutions. The Forums' purpose is to influence the political process in a more fundamental way. Before elected officials decide upon specific proposals, they need to know what kinds of initiatives the public favors. As President Carter once said, "Government cannot set goals and it cannot define our vision." The purpose of the Forums is to provide an occasion for people to decide what broad direction public action should take.

THE BOUNDARIES OF FREE SPEECH: HOW FREE IS TOO FREE?

One of the reasons people participate in the National Issues Forums is that they want leaders to know how they feel about the issues. So that we can present your thoughts and feelings about this issue, we'd like you to fill out this ballot before you attend Forum meetings (or before you read this book if you buy it elsewhere) and a second ballot after the Forum (or after you've read the material).

The moderator of your local Forum will ask you to hand in this ballot at the end of the session. If you cannot attend the meeting, send the completed ballot to National Issues Forums, 100 Commons Road, Dayton, Ohio 45459-2777.

1. Please indicate whether, over the last 10 years or so, the following has increased, stayed about the same, or decreased.

	Increased	Stayed the Same	Decreased	Not Sure
a. The amount of violent material on TV	☐	☐	☐	☐
b. The amount of sexually explicit material on TV	☐	☐	☐	☐
c. The amount of intolerant (e.g., racist, sexist, anti-gay or anti-Semitic) expression	☐	☐	☐	☐

2. How much effect do you think today's violent movies have in causing real violence?

Check One

a. Considerable	☐
b. Little	☐
c. Not sure	☐

3. The following questions are about pornography — books, movies, magazines, and photographs that show or describe sex activities. Please indicate if you think sexual materials do or do not have that effect.

	Yes	No	Not Sure
a. Sexual materials provide an outlet for bottled-up impulses	☐	☐	☐
b. Sexual materials lead people to commit rape	☐	☐	☐
c. Sexual materials lead to the breakdown of morals	☐	☐	☐
d. Sexual materials provide information about sex	☐	☐	☐

4. Please indicate whether you agree or disagree.

	Agree	Disagree	Not Sure
a. There is too much violence on television these days	☐	☐	☐
b. There is too much sex on television these days	☐	☐	☐

5. A judge in Florida has ruled that some lyrics of the rap group 2 Live Crew are so violent and sexually explicit as to be obscene. Those who sell or perform this music now face prosecution. In your own community, do you think such music should be:

Check One

a. Available to any buyer	☐
b. Available only to adult buyers	☐
c. Available to any buyer but with a warning label	☐
d. Not available	☐
e. Not sure	☐

(over)

6. For each of the following forms of speech or expression indicate whether you think it should be: (1) Officially banned by the government, (2) Privately restricted (relying on the judgment of radio and TV stations, publishers, newsstand owners, college and university administrators, etc.) but *not* restricted by the government, or (3) Not restricted by the government or private organizations but left up to the individual's judgment.

	Officially Banned	Privately Restricted	Not Restricted
a. Groups like the Ku Klux Klan having their own cable TV show	☐	☐	☐
b. Unusually sexually explicit, unedited movies on network TV like *Body Heat* or *9 1/2 Weeks*	☐	☐	☐
c. Unusually violent, unedited movies on network TV like *The Texas Chainsaw Massacre* or *Total Recall*	☐	☐	☐
d. Magazines like *Playboy* or *Penthouse*	☐	☐	☐
e. Songs with unusually violent or sexually explicit lyrics played on the radio	☐	☐	☐
f. Songs with unusually violent or sexually explicit lyrics sold in record stores	☐	☐	☐
g. Comedians like Andrew Dice Clay whose material is sexually explicit or racially offensive appearing on TV	☐	☐	☐
h. Shouting racist remarks in a public place such as the center of a college campus	☐	☐	☐
i. Male students engaging in sexist harassment or shouting obscenities on a college campus	☐	☐	☐

7. Which of these statements comes closest to your feelings about laws on unusually violent, sexually explicit, or intolerant (racist, sexist) language?

Check One

a. The government should officially restrict unusually violent, sexually explicit, or intolerant expression OR ☐

b. Such expression should be privately restricted (relying on the judgment of radio and TV stations, publishers and newsstand owners, colleges and universities, etc.) but *not* by the government OR ☐

c. Unusually violent, sexually explicit, or intolerant expression should not be restricted, but individuals should be free to voice their moral disapproval of such expression OR ☐

d. Not sure ☐

8. Which of these age groups are you in?

☐ Under 18 ☐ 18-29 ☐ 30-44 ☐ 45-65 ☐ Over 65

9. Are you a ☐ Man ☐ Woman

10. What is your ZIP CODE? _____

THE BOUNDARIES OF FREE SPEECH: HOW FREE IS TOO FREE?

Now that you've had a chance to read the book or attend a Forum discussion we'd like to know what you think about this issue. Your opinions, along with those of thousands of others who participated in this year's Forums, will be reflected in a summary report prepared for participants as well as elected officials and policymakers working on this problem. Since we're interested in whether you have changed your mind about certain aspects of this issue, the questions are the same as those you answered earlier.

Please hand this ballot to the Forum leader at the end of the session, or mail it to National Issues Forums, 100 Commons Road, Dayton, Ohio 45459-2777.

1. Please indicate whether, over the last 10 years or so, the following has increased, stayed about the same, or decreased.

	Increased	Stayed the Same	Decreased	Not Sure
a. The amount of violent material on TV	☐	☐	☐	☐
b. The amount of sexually explicit material on TV	☐	☐	☐	☐
c. The amount of intolerant (e.g., racist, sexist, anti-gay or anti-Semitic) expression	☐	☐	☐	☐

2. How much effect do you think today's violent movies have in causing real violence?

Check One

a. Considerable ☐
b. Little ☐
c. Not sure ☐

3. The following questions are about pornography — books, movies, magazines, and photographs that show or describe sex activities. Please indicate if you think sexual materials do or do not have that effect.

	Yes	No	Not Sure
a. Sexual materials provide an outlet for bottled-up impulses	☐	☐	☐
b. Sexual materials lead people to commit rape	☐	☐	☐
c. Sexual materials lead to the breakdown of morals	☐	☐	☐
d. Sexual materials provide information about sex	☐	☐	☐

4. Please indicate whether you agree or disagree.

	Agree	Disagree	Not Sure
a. There is too much violence on television these days	☐	☐	☐
b. There is too much sex on television these days	☐	☐	☐

5. A judge in Florida has ruled that some lyrics of the rap group 2 Live Crew are so violent and sexually explicit as to be obscene. Those who sell or perform this music now face prosecution. In your own community, do you think such music should be:

Check One

a. Available to any buyer ☐
b. Available only to adult buyers ☐
c. Available to any buyer but with a warning label ☐
d. Not available ☐
e. Not sure ☐

(over)

6. For each of the following forms of speech or expression indicate whether you think it should be: (1) Officially banned by the government, (2) Privately restricted (relying on the judgment of radio and TV stations, publishers, newsstand owners, college and university administrators, etc.) but *not* restricted by the government, or (3) Not restricted by the government or private organizations but left up to the individual's judgment.

	Officially Banned	Privately Restricted	Not Restricted
a. Groups like the Ku Klux Klan having their own cable TV show	☐	☐	☐
b. Unusually sexually explicit, unedited movies on network TV like *Body Heat* or *9 1/2 Weeks*	☐	☐	☐
c. Unusually violent, unedited movies on network TV like *The Texas Chainsaw Massacre* or *Total Recall*	☐	☐	☐
d. Magazines like *Playboy* or *Penthouse*	☐	☐	☐
e. Songs with unusually violent or sexually explicit lyrics played on the radio	☐	☐	☐
f. Songs with unusually violent or sexually'explicit lyrics sold in record stores	☐	☐	☐
g. Comedians like Andrew Dice Clay whose material is sexually explicit or racially offensive appearing on TV	☐	☐	☐
h. Shouting racist remarks in a public place such as the center of a college campus	☐	☐	☐
i. Male students engaging in sexist harassment or shouting obscenities on a college campus	☐	☐	☐

7. Which of these statements comes closest to your feelings about laws on unusually violent, sexually explicit, or intolerant (racist, sexist) language?

Check One

a. The government should officially restrict unusually violent, sexually explicit, or intolerant expression OR ☐

b. Such expression should be privately restricted (relying on the judgment of radio and TV stations, publishers and newsstand owners, colleges and universities, etc.) but *not* by the government OR ☐

c. Unusually violent, sexually explicit, or intolerant expression should not be restricted, but individuals should be free to voice their moral disapproval of such expression OR ☐

d. Not sure ☐

8. Which of these age groups are you in?

☐ Under 18 ☐ 18-29 ☐ 30-44 ☐ 45-65 ☐ Over 65

9. Are you a ☐ Man ☐ Woman

10. What is your ZIP CODE? _____